Praise for *Late Work*

"The work of the writer, late and soon, is life itself . . . it's that simple, that diffi-cult. Through analogy and example, Joan Frank's essays take us with her into a dimming world: to look, to feel, to cherish and forgive. This is a rich, real col-lection." | Carol Sklenicka, author of *Alice Adams: Portrait of a Writer*

"*Late Work* is one of the best books on writing and the writing life I have ever read. It contains wonderful pages about the covenant between writer and reader along with advice for writers on how to use one's own 'skinlessness' as a creative tool. It is above all a book about art and the role, both tempering and freeing, that aging plays in an artist's life and work." | Joel Agee, author of *The Stone World*

"Joan Frank defines art as truth, so that's what she shares in this autobi-ographical collection of craft essays. *Late Work* lays bare a dedicated writer's reflections about the value of art and her experiences publishing literary books while readership declines and the industry rarely champions literary work. Personal assessments are made, a fundamental truth gives direction, and this literary artist's calling abides." | Nan Cuba, founder of Gemini Ink and author of *Body and Bread: A Novel*

"Samuel Beckett once wrote, 'You must go on. I can't go on. I'll go on.' The author of *Late Work* signals to us from the passing lane of the long-haul high-way. She writes because someone is reading. To that, I'd add that someone is writing. Joan Frank is. Still." | Alison Moore, author of *Riders on the Orphan Train*

"Joan Frank's assessment of lateness as a conduit of possibility—by which, reading and writing, we record the subtle and continuous miracle of being alive—makes this a wise and moving book." | Debra Monroe, author of *My Unsentimental Education*

"*Late Work* gets to the heart of how a mature writer makes work that matters. At once wry, generous, and brutally honest, it is an essential guide for serious writers and readers of all ages." | Yang Huang, author of *My Good Son: A Novel*

Late Work

Also by Joan Frank

late work

A Literary Autobiography of
Love, Loss, and What I Was Reading

Joan Frank

University of New Mexico Press | Albuquerque

Library of Congress Cataloging-in-Publication Data
Names: Frank, Joan, 1949– author.
Title: Late work : a literary autobiography of love, loss, and what I was reading /
  Joan Frank.
Description: Albuquerque : University of New Mexico Press, 2022.
Identifiers: LCCN 2022013266 (print) | LCCN 2022013267 (e-book) |
  ISBN 9780826364203 (paperback) | ISBN 9780826364210 (e-book)
Subjects: LCSH: Frank, Joan, 1949– | Authors, American—20th century—
  Biography. | BISAC: LITERARY COLLECTIONS / Essays | LANGUAGE
  ARTS & DISCIPLINES / Writing / General | LCGFT: Autobiographies.
Classification: LCC PS3606.R38 Z46 2022 (print) | LCC PS3606.R38 (e-book) |
  DDC 813/.6 [B]—dc23/eng/20220415
LC record available at https://lccn.loc.gov/2022013266
LC e-book record available at https://lccn.loc.gov/2022013267

Founded in 1889, the University of New Mexico sits on the traditional home-
lands of the Pueblo of Sandia. The original peoples of New Mexico—Pueblo,
Navajo, and Apache—since time immemorial have deep connections to the land
and have made significant contributions to the broader community statewide.
We honor the land itself and those who remain stewards of this land throughout
the generations and also acknowledge our committed relationship to Indigenous
peoples. We gratefully recognize our history.

Cover illustration adapted from photograph by Edrece Stansberry on Unsplash
Designed by Felicia Cedillos
Composed in Georgia 9.3/14.25

Everything now is for my late sister, Andrie

Also in memory:
Bob Fogarty, 1938–2021
John Carlson, 1951–2021

If I let myself, I could stare out the window all day.

—NANCY RAPPOLT

There is a land of the living and a land of the dead and the bridge is love, the only survival, the only meaning.

—THORNTON WILDER, *THE BRIDGE OF SAN LUIS REY*

Turn up the light: sing on,
sing: On.

—MARGARET ATWOOD, "LATE POEMS"

We are what we are, and within our limitations we have made our own efforts. They seem puny in the light of eternity, but they didn't at the time, and they weren't.

—FRANK O'CONNOR

Contents

Acknowledgments

The following pieces first appeared, in slightly different forms, in the below journals. I thank their editors:

The Writing Disorder: "Make It Go Away: Love, Loss, and What I Was Reading"

Talking Writing: "Ready or Not," "Your Baby's Ugly," and "You've Made It"

Big Other: "Naked Emperors"

Psychology Today: "The Late Work Bylaws"

New World Writing: "I Say It's Spinach"

AUTHOR: "The Action Figures Collection"

Tikkun: "Another Art"

Passages North: "What Would John Williams Do?"

I owe composer Scott Wheeler deepest gratitude for his generous friendship, inspiration, and support. Peg Alford Pursell has given unconditional love, editing wisdom, and counsel, as have Cornelia Nixon, Val and Terry Mulcaire, Thaisa Frank, Joe Mackall, Nan Cuba, Alison Moore, the San Francisco Bay Area literati (they know who they are), the Warren Wilson posse (likewise), and my beautiful family.

Above all I thank my beloved husband, Bob Duxbury, for a lifetime's patient, witty *abbondanza*.

Grateful admiration to Elise McHugh, Katherine White, James Ayers, Alexandra Hoff, Felicia Cedillos, and the wonderful team at the University of New Mexico Press.

Special thanks to Phillip Lopate, Debra Monroe, Yang Huang,

Introduction

These essays were written over the last approximately ten years. All of them grapple with events and issues notably endemic—though never limited to—writers who've been at it awhile.

I've always loved portraiture in art, and in special particular, self-portraits issuing from a period commonly categorized as Late Work. I love Rembrandt's aging face in self-portraits: that fierce, almost sublime comprehension, the infinitesimal inflections and perceptions, light-years removed from sentiment or vanity. When we think about Late Work in writing, we look to it for a similar, distilled essence. As time runs out, stakes for "getting it right" intensify: no returns come from squandering time on the inessential. This autumnal period—in all artistic media—compels and fascinates me.

Over time, an author learns things. But she also encounters unprecedented paradoxes, predicaments, ordeals: some involve intricacies of craft and some, sheer psychological survival. The author must invent her way through. It may go against Eastern philosophies to suggest that in work and in living I'm still vested in what a friend once called *never relinquishing the quest plot*. One's story is not over till it's over. Sometimes not even then. And when a thing happens to you for the first time—however much described elsewhere—it is news. Thus, it feels vitally urgent to tell this portion of the story—this finding oneself a member of the Late Work tribe—for what I am perceiving it to be.

In a review of a Cynthia Ozick novel, Lionel Shriver notes that its protagonist is "an imperfect man [whose] predicament is to have grown old. Having done so, he stands at the far edge of his life; to see anything at all, he must turn and look back. 'I think incessantly of death,' he writes, 'of oblivion, how nothing lasts, not even memory when the one who remembers is gone. And how can I go on with my memoir, to what end, for what purpose?'"

Shriver's stern rejoinder falls swiftly as a gavel: "Ozick knows to what end. She knows there is a relationship that begins within the writer and flows to the words she writes and on to her readers. 'Relation is reciprocity,' Buber wrote in *I and Thou.*"

Whatever we may think of Ozick or Shriver or even Buber, the above-named alchemy locates the marrow of literary life that seems endlessly to drive and seduce both writer and reader.

"How can I go on . . . to what end . . . for what purpose?"

The pieces that follow strive to respond.

What Would John Williams Do?

I t's a beautiful party on a beautiful hillside, a soft, midsummer after-
noon's dream. The lush ranch-style spread commands expansive
views: golden countryside rolling out below, warm and busy with a
faraway highway's ant-like movement of two-lane traffic, seeming to
imply for those of us lucky enough to be standing here, looking out at
it with our drinks and food—a kind of master-serenity. *We happy few.*

I'm pleased to spot an author I know, amid the chatting guests.

I present myself, glass of sparkling water in hand.

How're you doing, I ask.

Half an hour later, I wonder how soon I can get home to swallow a
handful of the Ativan my husband keeps in his suitcase, for when he
takes plane flights.

This author begins at once to report—to itemize—rampant writerly
success. Travel, publication, money. Most recently, this person's latest novel has snagged a top-tier agent who has wasted no time selling
it to an excellent publisher, for a cool high-five figure.

"I wanted six figures," concedes the smiling author. "But my agent
tells me that after foreign rights are sold, I'll have my six figures."

This person's prior novel is still selling. There's still money coming
in from it, "not a lot, but it is still coming": another achievement of
which this author, standing tall and smiling and smiling, is warmly
proud.

Finally, after the nonstop barrage of seamless triumph, the author
pauses:

"So what're *you* doing?"

I swallow. Feeling as though I'm in a Kristen Wiig film, in fact Wiig herself, thinking *Oh, why not just let this go where it's clearly heading, straight to the heart of hell,* I tell the truth. I am completing a new book while trying passionately to place (never mind "sell") the prior book, which was finished three years ago: a work continually declined with lavish, rueful compliments, because it is, according to the decliners, too quiet and interior.

This person shakes a shiny, attractive head.

"Joan, you're a beautiful writer. But you need to write *more commercially.*"

The author locks eyes with me, smiling on and on.

"Have a *male protagonist.* That's the secret." The author's brows bear down.

"And make *more stuff* happen. Lots more stuff."

"Write a book that anyone can recommend to anyone," adds this author, in a tone I can only categorize as one of suave, airy certainty.

Desperate to peel myself from this scalding surface, staring like a skinned rabbit into the *dare-you-to-deny-it* of that immutable, toothpaste-ad smile, I change the subject. I know this author organizes a writing conference every spring. I bring up the topic of that conference, offering to speak there as a guest panelist or presenter.

The author shakes the same shining head, explaining that it is necessary to invite Pulitzer winners as guest speakers, both to lure potential applicants and to justify charging a fairly hefty application fee (which pays the speakers' airfares).

"I'm sorry. You're not famous enough," murmurs the author. In a hastened appending of assumed humility, the author laughs: "*I'm* not famous enough."

———

Here's a word that, among writers, is spoken softly when it's spoken at all.

Ambition.

It's a bomb-like subject. Tim Parks argues, in a blog for the *New*

York Review of Books, that writers write as if to win a game. That's one premise. Lee Upton, in her brilliant essay collection *Swallowing the Sea"* offers a more complicated, multipronged study, suggesting that ambition keeps us alive and fertile as artists, audacious as explorers and adventurers:

> The aim of ambition is what matters. We have to decide how to fill the concept and what form our relationship to ambition may take. . . . To write imaginatively is to be a student of ambition, our own and that of our characters. . . . And what is ambition, for all its bad reputation, but the antithesis of death, the opposite of the undefended corpse? . . . I wouldn't want to deny ambition to any writer, including myself.

I can't pretend to have ever finally settled the questions: *What kind of ambition drives me? How much—if any, ever—is too much?*

And the toughest corollary:

Why?

Many writers style themselves as larger or deeper than the forces of ambition—as if they are listening to a nobler music, with eyes on the higher prize of "purest" artistic integrity.

This effort—this story—comforts us intermittently. But it's always under attack.

We see that some of the best artists since forever, exempting a remarkable few, remain furiously ambitious. "I've sacrificed everything. *Everything*," intoned T. C. Boyle.

I believe him. The commerce of art makes it so.

Ancient news? Right. Yet we seem to keep needing to unpack it, to clarify for ourselves our chosen policy, our position—to figure it out. And soon, to figure it out again. And again. The late, tormented, too-soon-gone Lucy Grealy wrote:

> I used to think truth was eternal, that once I knew, once I saw, it would be with me forever, a constant by which everything else could be measured. I know now that this isn't so, that most truths

are inherently unretainable, that we have to work hard all our lives to remember the most basic things.

I sometimes find this reality soothing—at other times, exhausting. It means writers have to start over daily from scratch. We have to remake the covenant, recraft the mission statement. We have to drop the noise and gestures—certainly the cocktail conversation—and square off with the come-to-Jesus bottom lines:

Work hard to make art.

Work hard to get art seen, and taken.

Work hard, at the same time, to remember why.

Perversely, I also hope that ambition can mean *seizing as many chances as possible to be generous*, to help those whose work we admire and care about. Why? Because one does as one hopes, eventually, to be done to. Because artistic solidarity has power. (Think of The Authors' Guild, PEN, and similar groups.) And frankly, because this mindset reverses and elevates what can otherwise too easily start to feel like the walk and talk of a roving mob of thugs.

The best artists made you feel that the best of them was at stake—didn't they?

A *New Yorker* profile (by Nick Paumgarten) of the much-lauded, late James Salter (then alive and nearing age ninety) noted that Salter had once made lists of those names he felt to be "ahead" of him en route to—no other way to say this—the level of greatness he meant to attain. Until then, I'd never imagined the tight-lipped Salter capable of that kind of calculation. Later, I understood it better in terms of the life Salter led (and described in his writing), mandated to experience the very best of everything: women, friendships, food and drink, travel, real estate, and physical-spiritual transport beyond mere sport—rock climbing, skiing, sex, piloting fighter aircraft during war. Though few of us maintain a to-do list like his, it calms me, oddly, to think that even the mighty Salter once smarted and chafed like trillions of other writers. Even the giants, it appears, nurse an all-too-human need.

But while that awareness can temporarily ease and even amuse—it does little else. The rest is up to us. Day after day each of us must finesse, revisit, and re-finesse her own mythology.

How we came to it. Why we stay.

After many years it seems clear to me that to write literary fiction, remain obscure on that radar, and still have ambition is not at all an unusual combination. It's just a statistically doomed one. Lee Upton: "There is something especially compelling about writers' ambitions, coming as they so often do—in actuality, despite labor and talent— apparently to nothing." Thus, no matter how often we've reasoned them out in the past, the same questions flash into our faces like vexing paparazzi bulbs we must push past—*Why do I do this? How should I do this? What does the former mean for the latter?*—sometimes fanned to a firewall in scenes like mine with the blissfully monomaniacal author at the fancy party.

I can only guess that the answers writers dig for, each time, have to feel real to us. They have to come from the no-escape, all-makeup-scrubbed-off, 3:00 a.m. dark of us.

My own personal measure for the realness of that answer—and let me emphasize the scorched-earth pain that drives the unsparingness of this search—is to ask myself how the late John Williams, author of the now-classic-but-once-unknown, quiet, perfect, devastating novel *Stoner* (on which, more later in this volume) might have answered if someone had locked eyes with him at a party and told him that he needed to write more commercially in order to become better known, and to make a pile of money.

Never mind that the protagonist of *Stoner* is a man, or the fact that quite a lot of "stuff" happens in Williams's heart-spearing novel—from Stoner's journey as a farm boy to the cataclysmic sea-change wreaked in him by a poem recited in a college English class, to a soul-killing marriage, estrangement from a beloved daughter, a hexed-but-vitalizing love affair, and finally a silent, self-aware, unheralded death. The novel's arc feels—like all our very greatest art—inevitable. Its particulars shine with the relevance of the universal. It is timeless.

What would John Williams say to my wealthy and self-satisfied interlocutor?

Nothing.

I'll bet he would say nothing at all. He might nod slightly. Then he would immediately excuse himself (as I finally summoned the wits to do) and vanish. (I don't know that Williams would go looking for Ativan, or its then-equivalent, alcohol. I skipped those options, too, and wound up having take-out dinner and renting a movie with my husband.)

Williams would, I'm pretty sure, carry on with his life, and with the writing he felt he had to do. Like his own stoic William Stoner, his work might be ignored, even mocked. He most certainly would have mulled his own motives now and again, perhaps doubting, even despairing. He would carry on. I don't know how much money Williams made. I'm sure he liked money fine when it came, as we all do. I'm sure he liked paying bills, buying food and books. I'm sure he was never fooled about the money's significance.

It's of course easy to idolize artists like Williams—and by now you'll have realized that for Williams's name we may substitute the name of any writer we've admired across the years, dead or living, who quietly persisted at making work that matters. The idolizing, and the little disturbances that prompt it, must also ultimately fall away, become part of the noise and the gestures, what a gifted poet friend calls "barking and scratching." Lee Upton reminds us: "There's another form of ambition that writers may focus on: the ambition to make a lifetime's work that adds to the sum of what Wallace Stevens, referring to poetry, called one of the 'enlargements of life.'" The only choice left is to decide for the work repeatedly—to rekindle, enact, embody hour by hour, what writers like Williams knew. As Lucy Grealy noted so shockingly simply, you have to work hard, every day, to remember.

The Late Work Bylaws

M uch is often made, in art, of what people call The Late Work. That first article announcing this solemn designation—the *The*—is important. It heralds a category: a singular section of a set trajectory. Think Rembrandt, Beethoven, Edna O'Brien, Toni Morrison. Also think O'Keeffe, Gehry, Varda; photographers, filmmakers, conductors, musicians, sculptors. (Wayne Thiebaud, to the end at age 101, worked every day.)

Our attitudes toward this category tend to blur it over with reverence—like some shrouding, numinous mist.

We assume that if an artist is older, by natural accrual and assimilation of experience they'll be likely to understand more. In short, they've had more time to get smart. We assume age gives wisdom, and also (with literature, music, sculpture, theater, or film) the ability to convey that wisdom with a more distilled beauty.

Burnished is a favorite descriptor for that beauty—also handy for evoking autumn, the color of expensive liquor and furniture, or the dull glow from ancient magic lanterns when you summon their resident genie.

As to wisdom? One of its most vaunted symptoms (I'm old enough now to speak for the population) may be an urge to downsize. We aging types feel driven, almost animalistically, to drop or cut away everything un-useful: emotional, physical, even intellectual baggage.

A sudden awareness of shrinking time has a striking way (paraphrasing Dr. Johnson) of clearing the mind. We move with speed to preserve what's working and toss the rest—never mind politeness and social noise. It means actively cleaning out the immediate house of the daily, choosing what's still needed, and dumping the rest—whatever's irrelevant, or just bums us out.

Of course, this includes people.

One phenomenon that stands out for surviving this ruthless process, I think, is a particular kind of friendship—if we're lucky, more than one. These we protect and tend like a kitchen garden: they're nourishment we need to live, different from spousal and partner relations.

Seldom, of course, do these friendships show up at the door fully formed. Like everything else, they evolve, often improbably or weirdly. I've made a couple of golden friends because one of us wrote the other a fan letter. (Letter-writing, via email, turns out to be my favorite expression of friendship. A good thing, too—during our COVID era, email letters have given many of us something close to psychic salvation.)

The caveat about the care and feeding of late-life friendships?

Idiosyncrasy.

No single friendship offers some wholesome, polished model. Most could be judged by any reasonable observer as strange, even eccentric. Each stipulates a secret recipe: attention must be paid, but in a fine-tuned way. Some friends touch base cheerfully every five or ten years, taking right up (at every level) where they left off. Others feel wounded if they've not heard back from you after more than a day (I've been that person). Writers are introverts by nature, who also live and die by language. When we actually *want* to reach out, every syllable exchanged, every nuance of every line, counts uber-heavily—during the Late Work, more so. On loyalty, we rely. An abrupt change of tone from an adored correspondent can feel to a writer like getting shot—at the very least like a pulled gun. Ask around.

But losing touch, too, consciously or not, has advantages; a natural attrition that simplifies. Reviewing a biography of the late poet Louise Bogan (one of her greatest poems is "Song for the Last Act"), the ever-wise William Maxwell observed:

[Bogan's] friendships were important to her, but as she grew older she felt less and less need for human company. People who wanted to see her for one reason or another—because they loved her or admired her or in some important way felt forever indebted to her—were usually put off with postponements or "visits to the dentist" too consistent to be plausible.

At this stage, you keep a friendship for something it gives: comfort, support, stimulation, shared history, laughs. (Some may enjoy sparring and bickering—that's a separate camp.) Why does this intrigue me? Because it's so purely chosen. Like growing flowers. Nobody requires it. Status doesn't depend on it. What's gained is real but not exactly palpable. During the Late Work, friendship's rarely about money, possessions, sex, or fame. It can certainly feel romantic, even erotic in terms of exuberance and wit; in terms of a delicious sense of brink-of-meaning—a rush; a heightened state; what a friend calls *heated agreement*. But the connections we keep—people we still want to bother spending time with—deliver. Knowing and feeling known, seeing and feeling seen: the prizes, the grail. True, ego's woven in: who doesn't love hearing *you're terrific*? But overall, these late attachments seem most defined by an understanding.

At the same time, each friendship carries its own seeds of self-destruction: boredom, irreconcilable viewpoints, sore issues, distraction. Some late friendships lose steam, roll off into a ditch, and die. Some burst into flame (ignited by a remark or act) and never recover. Some manage to resume but in a cautious, tiptoeing mode, relinquishing their original closeness and intensity, creating a surface détente.

These shifts and drifts can occur wordlessly and often carry a deep, unspoken sadness. Both sides know what happened. Both know the issues are too raw to be discussed. Both grieve the lost mainline of heated agreement. Love abides—but the daily adventure has been forfeited.

I have written a novel about one such friendship, between two women who are antithetical in type—like mirror-opposite sisters in a fairy tale—begun in high school and lasting for decades (*The Outlook for Earthlings*). Their oppositeness manifests, while each matures and makes choices, as a constant hurdle. They try their best to work around it. But like any human interaction, it can't stand still. Stakes, of course, loom high. We want our best friends to want what we want—at least to want it *for us*, right?

Clashing needs and values can hijack love between friends, as it does in *Earthlings*. That impasse isn't always age-related. But the pain of it bears special sharpness with age, again, because of the ticking clock, and awareness of finite resources. How much longer have we got each other? How do we want to see it out?

You won't hear me offering smart, snappy solutions here, any more than you'd expect solutions to weather (solutions to *normal* weather, that is, which may not, indeed, be a frequent visitor anymore). Fiction's job has never been to "solve," but rather to show us ourselves. We may feel trapped, even hogtied by a complicated friend. We may feel stabbed by that friend—or believe the friend is stabbing herself, as in *Earthlings,* when one woman can't fathom—or endorse—the near-masochistic thrall the other stubbornly maintains for a married lover:

> To loathe someone precisely for their goodness—blinkered, archaic, even pathological—was like stoning a gentle animal. How could anyone sustain such a stance?
>
> But was it really, at its heart, goodness? Or was it a choice to manifest the best possible facsimile of goodness? And what did that hide? And how honest was such hiding?
>
> All of this, inarticulable.
>
> Easy to say *I am glad you are happy.* Harder by far, it seemed, to cheer the apparatus of happiness.
>
> Mel insisted she was happy. Scarlet didn't buy it. Some fat lie lay coiled like a python in the engine room of that story.

Here is where the "keep or dump" standard falls off a cliff.

According to the Late Work bylaws, we should be sidestepping anguish, dusting our hands of ordeals; cutting losses. Time's a-wastin'! Yet some bonds do beg to transcend that. Some friendships wind up being "grandfathered in," as my husband puts it, simply because for all their quirkiness, they've been around that damned long. Like Robert Frost's definition of home: "when you go there, they have to take you in." Though these can cost us—sometimes quite badly—they've somehow become part of us, beyond judgment. No doubt I'm myself the beneficiary of somebody's grandfather clause (just as surely, my name's been quietly cut from someone's active-contacts list).

We're forced, ultimately, to rethink the rules of Late Work. Who gets to stay in the ring with us during what precious time remains? How do we make sense of that?

Here's a thought. We can behave, finally, like one of those Google Earth cameras.

We can pan back—far, far back, far as you like—say to some spot out in the galaxy that affords a nice, vast view: the planets and stars but also (however you envision this) the infinite surge of time, and pinpointed somewhere along that, the hair-slender bandwidth we humans take up on its spectrum.

With this breathtaking vista before the mind's eye we must, I believe—almost as a commandment—try to forgive everybody.

Parents, children, friends, enemies. Monsters, saints—almost everybody—as best we can, even if all we can manage is a quiet aware-ness of our own struggle to do this. Something easeful is released when thinking is rerouted this way, no?

Never least, we must try to forgive ourselves, singly and collec-tively.

Agreed: Hella hard. Full disclosure: I fail at it regularly. I've behaved badly, in ways I'm still trying to grasp. Also, few humans can forgive anybody, or even want to. Plenty of deceased artists, old or not at the hour of departure, have gone straight into that good night bitterly raging—less against the night than against some petty insult or slight.

We are free to elect to be an idiot or an ass until the last breath.

And: mental travel into deep space may require strenuous practice.

But: tick tock.

Recall the much-quoted poem, Raymond Carver's "Late Fragment:"

And did you get what
you wanted from this life, even so?
I did.
And what did you want
To call myself beloved, to feel myself
beloved on the earth.

"The quality of mercy is not strained." It's a line I've always loved, with its analogy to rain. Rain. Why not resolve to let mercy wash through us, during Late Work's enterprises, to include our bizarre, beloved friends? This need not mean sticky sentiment: maybe instead, a way of seeing that *denies no worst thing.* (Look into Rembrandt's eyes in those last self-portraits, if you doubt this.) Why not let mercy be the lens, the call and response we sing, however softly, somewhere toward the end?

Lifeness Itself: Divining the Details

"No inanimate object . . . in a story or a novel is arbitrary."

—ALICE MCDERMOTT

Some of us have so little patience for fussy particulars that we finish people's sentences for them. Similarly, our skin crawls when we listen to finicky self-correction. "It was Tuesday—no, Saturday. They ate fish—wait, it was pasta."

But we seem to have all the time in the world for the billion tiny, careful stitches of detail in Tolstoy's blazing tapestries. (In *War and Peace*, a certain aging dignitary had a habit of *pressing people's hands* when he took them into his own.)

We inhale the specifics in E. B. White: "the smell of manure"; "the back of a baby's neck when its mother keeps it tidy"; or the moment when White watches his then-young stepson tug on a pair of cold, wet swim trunks and *feels* that cold in his own groin.

These details seem to construct the work, brick by brick. At the same time, they do worlds more than brick-duty. They crackle with voltage; they project a force field.

So why, then, when other writers plunge into itemizing rooms, objects and surfaces, mannerisms or weather, do we begin to itch and grow bored, even angry? When does our appetite for details, as readers, start to cramp? Why does a level of detail used by one writer seem unforgettable—even ravishing—yet in other hands start to feel pointless, superfluous, dull?

Why do some authors deliver something radiant, voluptuous, and memorable with their details, while others leave us readers feeling *conned* once we have waded through?

We've all experienced it. Readers invest more than time in a story: we invest memory. We sense that if we hold certain details in mind they will eventually feel justified, or at least accounted for, and in a best case, pay us back in some way. A kind of coming-together-of-it-all will arrive that will *make it make sense* for us to have kept track. Above all, we invest emotion. Readers are wonderfully willing to give a writer every benefit of doubt, to empathize and be patient. But if we start to suspect that *nothing will reward or answer* our patience— after we've collected and sorted all that highly particular information—we feel handled. Anger may follow. The book is scuttled; the reader soured, disappointed, often baffled.

If we readers find ourselves asking a work, *Why are you telling me this*, the writing's in trouble.

Of course, I need not remind you how high stakes have become for reader attention. That's why it's almost impossible for a piece of writing to survive once any reader's mind reaches that moment of *enough: who cares*.

It's a high bar, and—brutally—pretty much the first bar.

What's trickier still is that we must try here to push aside issues of taste and aesthetics while unpacking the riddle of detail, because getting caught up in taste and aesthetics can derail us. People can grow defensive and emotional defending their own tastes; they can get sidetracked trying to "win" an argument about literary merit (forgetting they share, first and last, a love of reading).

Also—complicatingly—tastes and aesthetics change. Younger readers, for example, tend not to care much about lengthy descriptions of landscapes. Whereas older readers—I'm speaking generally now—tend to gobble down every pebble and raindrop. Why? I would suggest it's because those details are *markers of the recognized, cherished world in perceived time*. Time—and every infinitesimal thing that time is stuffed with—becomes more precious as the amount of it available to us shrinks. People's perceptions change as they age. They want to slow time down; to really *look* at things.

On the other hand: A close friend, a reverent and lifelong reader, told me she has no qualms about skimming over long, descriptive passages in even the most respected works—say the tour of Paris sewers in *Les Miserables*. She likes to cut to the human interaction. That's what interests her. So she skips elaborate descriptions without a speck of guilt. Other details, however, she hungers for and lingers over: nuances of characters' thoughts, gestures, conversations.

Why? Because, she'd answer, of the sensibility they convey.

By *sensibility* I will use Sven Birkerts's definition: "a cluster of values and the mentality they help manifest." Of course readers need not *like* a sensibility, or identify with it, to be spellbound by it. Think of *Lolita's* Humbert Humbert, or the smooth Porfiry Petrovich, who slowly, methodically, almost *affectionately* closes in on poor Raskolnikov in *Crime and Punishment*.

Details convey sensibility, and not just an author's or a character's. *Objects and conditions in prose contain their own life—enriching and powering the story's life.* So our choice of them, our use of them, matters passionately. Here's Charles Baxter, from his (rightfully) revered essays, *Burning Down the House*: "Objects are being forced to go to work, carrying lunch pails, putting their shoulders to the wheel—they are being *employed* as a literary workforce to carry their burden of human feeling."

Literary critic James Wood adds (italics are mine):

[It] can be said that the [life] of a story *lies in its details.* . . . I think of details as nothing less than bits of life sticking out of the frieze of form, imploring us to touch them. Details are not, of course, just bits of life: they represent that magical fusion, . . . whereby artifice is . . . converted into . . . life. Details are not lifelike but irreducible: things-in-themselves, what I would call *lifeness itself.*

Proust's famous madeleine may be the most notorious example of detail's power. Henry James called it "palpable intimacy."

———

Thus: good details work in two ways. First, they embody the whole work's essence, like seeds or bio-samples. Second, they emit energy that pushes the narrative along like oxygenated blood.

We can also suggest that details act like a trail of crumbs leading readers deeper into the story's world—except each crumb is also numinous. They don't just point the way or drag us along: they glow in the dark; they pulsate with spiritual density. And this happens (paradoxically) because of their realness, their concreteness.

Our earliest perception of meaning comes through the senses. "You hear a big bang in childhood," notes author Thaisa Frank (no relation). First meanings are encoded into cellular memory: the smell of rain, the taste of milk, how light touches surfaces.

All our lives, our senses continue to register detail indelibly. In David Constantine's glittering novel, *The Life-Writer*, young Eric, hitchhiking through France, listens to stories of the First World War from a kind man (Bresson) who's given him a lift. At the end of their ride together:

> Eric thanked him, opened the car door, reached behind for his rucksack and made to get out. One last thing, said Bresson—un petit souvenir. I want to be remembered kindly by someone as old as I was when I went away from home into the first of the wars. He took a small cloth bag from the glove compartment. Hold out your hands, he said. Make a cup of them. And into that warm and containing space, out of the crimson pouch, in a glistening slither, he tipped a dozen, two dozen, three dozen small thin silver coins. Treasure, he said, from back then. Eric stared. . . . After a while Bresson held out the open pouch. Best pour them back in, he said. Eric made a chute of his hands and the coins like a shoal of flashing fish slid with a tinkling out of sight. Bresson drew the pouch shut and handed it back to him. For safekeeping, he said.

It's not too strong a claim to declare that good detail transfigures: the story becomes more than itself, told by more than words. It becomes a dimensional, self-sustaining myth. Objects inside the story radiate energy that knits it more tightly to itself—and to us. A strong story becomes part of us, carried like DNA.

Concrete detail need not reflect a character's feelings—it can often act *against* a character's feelings. (Baxter notes how, in Virginia Woolf's *To the Lighthouse*, weather creeps into an empty house and wants to destroy it.) Either way, details organize, deepen, enrich, charge, and energize the dream. Here's a passage from the novel *Time Present and Time Past* by Dierdre Madden, describing the interior of an old house:

> It was the strangest house she had ever seen . . . remarkably old-fashioned. It was all wainscoting and dark-green paint, hooked rugs and framed tapestries. There was a stuffed fish in fake weed, with the name of the lake where it had been caught painted in gold letters on the glass case. There was a black piano, and an old-fashioned gramophone with a great golden horn. Even though it was spring it was a cold day, and there had been a fire burning in the grate, and on the table there was a huge vase full of daffodils that blasted the room with their yellow energy; that lit the place up more than any lamp could ever have done. It had been like going back in time, like stumbling into the pages of a story book, so that . . . if the cat on the hearth—and there was always a cat, even back then—had sat up and spoken to her, she thought that she would hardly have been surprised.

So how about those daffodils? But everything else, too: the black piano, the gold letters describing where the stuffed fish was caught, the echoing gold in the "great golden horn" of the gramophone. Though we are just meeting this house, its props give such thick atmosphere, such a porous sense of history and possibility, we can fairly smell it. Madden's details prime us to anticipate: interesting things will happen here.

Sometimes it's pure idiosyncrasy that carries detail into our hearts. In Carson McCullers's *The Ballad of the Sad Cafe*, one character is hunchbacked, the other slightly cross-eyed. Often the more peculiar the detail, the more believable. Why? Because that's who we are. We are idiosyncrasy made flesh. We are highly, specifically bizarre. And art, finally, is about mapping that.

The late Robert Stone said, "There's only one subject for fiction or poetry or even a joke: how it is. In all the arts, the payoff is always the same: recognition. If it works, you say that's real, that's truth, that's life, that's the way things are."

By details, now, I mean more than just lists or listing. Lists can be delicious to make and to read, and many craft lectures focus upon them. But beware: lists can also feel busy, even come to oppress a reader. Using them too often or making them too long can feel like resorting to mattress-stuffing. So they must be deployed like spice: with timing and restraint.

To be very clear: by details I mean the judicious selection of facts, events, thoughts, conditions, settings, dialogue, but especially observed objects that vitalize the story.

The damnable thing, of course, is that no one can hand us a recipe for snagging best details. Instead, we investigate tactics for luring them.

One is, naturally, to study the writers we love very closely, comparing their details with those of others. How many, and what kind, show up in a given passage? What senses are addressed? Does eccentricity make them more powerful?

Sven Birkerts has noted that as readers, our minds "bustle about" building the world of a story. But it's a mistake to treat details as if they were glue or filler, to be shoveled or stuffed (wheel-spinning, waffling, pointless delay).

To locate detail that lives and breathes, the writer's job is first and always to let herself drop deeply into the dream. That's a hallowed space, and we all have our methods for getting there—the place where we keep quiet, trust the stillness, watch the opened clearing in the woods to see what creatures venture in. When they do, we start scribbling (or typing). A pulsing current of remembered or imagined images is something to trust and transcribe as fast as we can—never (at that point) forcing form onto it, not editing or correcting or even thinking about it too much.

Details emerge from the dream, along with everything else.

In one workshop I heard a student remark about another's story character: "She wears a wig and drives a van, and that is all we need to know."

———

Let's return briefly to the riddle of why one writer ignites us with detail, whereas others' particulars bore or even infuriate us.

As a book reviewer (mainly of literary fiction), I am struck repeatedly by the difference. Entering one novel by a writer I'd not previously encountered, I am standing right behind the narrator's shoulder: I smell the burnt pan on the stove, feel the heat seeping through the splintering porch stairs. At that moment, *I'm in*. But in another novel by a prominent author, I grow exasperated with the long, meticulous description of the high-fashion handbag the narrator's jilted fiancée has thrown at him.

Why? One bankable reason: the handbag felt *imposed*. It felt like *duty*.

What I'm about to say next may sound absurdly obvious. But often (perhaps overeager to assume complexity) we overlook the obvious. So please simply dwell with this not-grammatically-graceful idea:

Detail must feel *felt*.

You may have heard writers and teachers remark of someone's work: "It was a *felt story*." They mean the story embodied personal, emotional urgency—as though it could have been written with the author's blood.

For that to happen, the smallest particular must read as *felt*. It went into the writer's skin: now it's in yours. Palpable intensity jumps like a spark into your chest; reverberates in the fillings of your teeth. It will never feel like something pasted on, pumped painstakingly in, or sprinkled over.

I believe that this happens when a writer feels the details they use with the same current of urgency that their story is feeding them. Even if the vision in their mind is chaotic, the details come straight from that seething energy.

———

In James Agee's immortal, Pulitzer-winning *A Death in the Family*, a young father is wakened by a phone call in the wee hours summoning him to a family emergency. He eats the breakfast his devoted wife has risen to prepare for him. After he drives away she reenters their bedroom and sees with a shock of pleasure that *he has made the bed and turned the cover down on her side* to tempt her to return to sleep.

It tells us worlds about the couple, and their marriage.

Detail must feel part of the breath that blows the story into being.

We are also, as writers and editors, obeying laws of cadence. Writing is music in the reading ear.

Example: Poet and author Stephen Dobyns once responded to a story of mine in which I'd named a couple of items in a character's lunch—maybe an apple and a sandwich.

One more, Stephen scribbled into the margin. He meant: *You need one more item here.*

He was not just responding to the Rule of Three. He was urging me to finish the song. You hear the familiar, chestnut melody: "Shave and a haircut"—and then who can resist at least *thinking* the final notes of that musical phrase? "Two bits." We are talking now about rounding out rhythm, as well as depth, breadth, and texture, with detail: distilling the music of the writing with concision.

The works of James Salter or Simon Van Booy read, to me, like alpine water: clear, pure, crystalline. Their attention to detail is exquisite, but ultra-judicious. (Van Booy, in his novel *The Illusion of Separateness*, noted that an elementary school hallway "smelled of milk and coats.")

Charlie Baxter: "The things carry the feeling."

This happens, I re-remind you, because that same feeling drives the writer. Choosing felt detail becomes, like writing itself, a meditation—honed by practice.

We write to dig for something—often we don't know, until much later, what that is. And in the course of digging, certain details push up into view like bits of archaeological treasure. These bits help take us where we didn't know we needed to go. More oddly, they themselves often do the best telling. Listen to author Richard Bausch:

In an experiment in New York in the mid sixties, they asked elementary school children to draw their parents. [The kids] were too young to have any attitudes or opinions; they saw things directly from experience. They came up with the most amazing symbolic drawings: Dad's big as a barrel, with beer cans on his stomach; Mom's tiny, standing next to a Matterhorn of laundry. The details were vivid and stunningly revealing. This is what Flannery O'Connor is talking about when she says a good story is literal, in the same sense that a child's drawing is literal.

From this you take the faith that what you are really after in describing experience is to recover the direct gaze of the child, to be an infant with speech. The details will take care of themselves, if you can be, simply, straightly, clear. Forget everything you think you know and just try to be clear, try to render exactly what your direct gaze gives you to say.

Recover the direct gaze of the child. Forget everything you think you know and just try to be clear. Render what your gaze gives you to say. A writer's never-ending quest: *how it is.* God, and the devil—the how itself—are in the details.

I Say It's Spinach

"A novel is a set of strategies, closer to something in mathematics or quantum physics than something in ethics or sociology. It is a release of certain energies and a dramatization of how these energies might be controlled, given shape."

—COLM TÓIBÍN

"I wish that future novelists would reject the pressure to write for the betterment of society. We need novels that live . . . past the political agenda described on social media. We have imaginations for a reason. . . . We need characters in novels to be free to range into the dark and wrong. How else will we understand ourselves?"

—OTTESSA MOSHFEGH

A strange phenomenon is seeping into literary fiction. It's tricky to describe, tricky to understand; ultra-tricky to thwart or deflect. But it's no less disturbing for all that—a kind of elephant-in-the-room of contemporary fiction.

Because we now live on a planet in serious jeopardy, whose populations (especially the marginalized, oppressed, and disenfranchised) struggle to survive, to be seen and met—modern consciousness has become a great, surging shatter-belt of change.

In so many ways, that change is valiant.

Human rights—particularly rights of women, people of color, children, marginalized or fluid genders and sexualities, plants and animals, air and water—are on the one hand under attack, but on the other also being more rigorously noticed, championed, and defended than ever before. People are speaking truth to power lately—almost around the clock. And that's good.

But in the making of literary art here in America, I'm seeing a trend—putting this simply—to editorialize in the course of storytelling.

I began to notice it a few years ago, reviewing literary fiction. Novels and stories began to surface which contained, shall we say, an agenda.

They arrived bearing a Message, with a capital M.

These agendas varied. All tended to be passionate, ecological, humanitarian. They've been logical, moral, well intended.

But they've not been art.

I don't want to vilify individuals. But I can cite a few who are established enough that they won't suffer for being named here.

One I recall off the top of my head is British author Helen Simpson, well respected in America and the UK, whose story collection I reviewed some years ago. In one of those stories, a character refused to fly on airplanes because plane flight is ruining the biosphere. The character's refusal to fly disrupted a relationship she was having with a man who lived at some distance. Lengthy explanations floated forward, detailing this character's reasoning. And whenever that happened, the story and characters almost disappeared, becoming instead a delivery system for what were obviously Simpson's own powerful concerns.

As a reader and a reviewer, I felt alarmed. Something serious was at stake. Something vital was being derailed.

Let me pause again to underscore: *No agenda described here is unworthy, or not desperately important.* Quite the reverse. Of course these causes are important. They're real. They're beyond reproach— some even life-or-death urgent.

Nonetheless: *They are not the story.* Or if they are, they're not being conveyed that way. Bluntly? They're axes an author wishes to grind. And in my view, the insertion or injection or pasting-on of an

agenda, the blatant grinding of axes, highjacks and sabotages art—
often ham-handedly, however righteously—and in the end forfeits a
product that has potential to accomplish something much larger than
any sermonizing could or would.

Upshot: a writer shoots her art in the foot with her own good
intentions.

Awful effects of editorializing are multiple.

One is to make a work's Voice, capital V, melt away—just literally
evanesce—and be replaced by the author's personal or editorial voice,
what we might call the *Infomercial* Voice: like the voiceover for
civics-class films we had to watch in school. If a character opens her
mouth and what comes out is a pile of exposition in the tone and
mode of an educative pitch, she stabs the prose in the back. Gone is a
work's dimensional, idiosyncratic wholeness, its unique essence. Lost
is Grace Paley's famous *open destiny* of that character's life.

That breed of character is often called—uncharitably but
accurately—a "mouthpiece." When the authorial truck backs up and
dumps a pile of infomercial factoids in a reader's lap, that reader
quickly grasps that an author's agenda weighs more, in the telling,
than anything else—character or story. Balance and tone are chopped
up, occluded, cast out.

So are plausibility, believability, persuasiveness.

It's like watching an actor in a powerful, moving play who stops to
pull from his pocket a jar of marmalade. He turns directly to the audience and—breaking character—begins to rhapsodize in his private-life
voice about how much he adores that sweet-sour, orange-peel jam.

Except it's not marmalade we're talking here. It's Causes with a
capital C. Super-moral, super-valiant causes, but causes all the same.
Saving forests and water, protecting air, saving oppressed or suffering or underserved groups, the nation, civilization, the planet.

Please, please know I am hyperaware that these causes are excru-
ciatingly timely, necessary. Valid. Sincere.

But valid and sincere cannot be art's sole measure or criteria.

I know I open myself up for attack.

First, I'm a well-educated white woman—with access to enough food, shelter, and mortal safety to have the luxury and autonomy of being able to consider such questions.

Second, no one of sound mind doubts whether these causes need champions and support.

Third (my attackers may argue), how can we as a species bother with art if we and the planet are not first alive and well? How can art matter if we're in flames or drowning?

On the face of it, these objections are logical. But I must insist that *art that is art*—at least in terms of literary fiction—*wants nothing to do with lobbyists.*

Art, by definition, gets things said in forms dictated by its own vision, what we might call a framed totality—an organism embodying realities that may *involve* Causes, but never propagandizes for them. Causes may permeate form but they must feel inseparable from a story's very tissue.

Think of the heart-stabbing scene in *War and Peace* in which the innocent young Petya Rostov—a boy who has romanticized a soldier's life and longs to be a military hero—has been allowed to stand with the mounted ranks on the sidelines of battle in the Napoleonic Wars, in the care of a trusted family friend. On enthralled impulse, Petya rides into battle against orders—and is almost instantly killed. The moment is offered matter-of-factly, which renders it the more shattering. I think, too, of Anne Michaels's indelible first novel *Fugitive Pieces*, in which a starving Greek geologist saves a war orphan during the reign of fascism by smuggling the terrified child in his coat to his home on a Greek island. I think of Mohsin Hamid's astonishing *Exit West*—a tour de force placing a reader inside a nameless, possibly Middle Eastern city torn from within and without by warring factions, juxtaposing modern realities with heinous, near-medieval-style slayings. Did Tolstoy or Michaels or Hamid pause mid-prose to announce, "Hey, listen up, people. War is very bad for living things!" (In fact Tolstoy *did* editorialize for religious convictions in a coda to *War and Peace* and elsewhere. But when he did that, it failed horribly. And in *War and Peace*'s main body, fortunately for the human race, story triumphs.)

Some may argue that, given the nature of modern problems, it can't any longer be possible to separate Cause and Story.

To which I say: art gets done what it needs to get done—but *Cause must be jettisoned as Cause, per se.*

Story, in other words, must drive everything but also irradiate it. A story gathers and chews up and assimilates whatever it needs—issuing itself in a form, each time, that insists upon its own content. What's consistent is that art privileges the wholeness of the story or vision, which is to say, truthful complexity. Cause tends by definition to simplify, to present a seamless, blemish-free facade, like—well, like propaganda. Cause will airbrush complexity right out of the picture, given half a chance. Cause resists built-in contradictions, shadows, crosscurrents, exceptions, ironies, paradoxes, and similar mitigating elements.

Thus, art takes the longer view but also uses human magnification. Writers like Jhumpa Lahiri or Akhil Sharma have given us the experience of the children of first-generation émigrés—replete with difficulty, pain, egos, vindictiveness, aggression, loneliness, fear, greed, lust, striving—James Wood's notorious "lifeness itself."

Denis Johnson gives us addicts and inmates; Toni Morrison, life and death in Black America. Dorothy Allison gives us a child at the mercy of abusive family. Rebecca West, in *The Fountain Overflows*, gives us a father who is brilliant and doting yet terribly, even fatally, flawed. Jesmyn Ward gives us a struggling Black family torn further asunder by a hurricane. Rachel Kushner's *The Mars Room* gives a masterful tour of life inside (and outside) a women's prison. And in Matthew Thomas's deeply absorbing novel *We Are Not Ourselves*, as well as in Joshua Henkins's *Morningside Heights*, two exemplary fathers succumb slowly to Alzheimer's. But never, *ever* do we feel, in the course of the above stories, that we are reading a recital of statistics, of soapboxing, or bandwagoning. These stories simply carry us away with authentic complexity and (therefore) authority, entering us to live.

Assigned to review Ali Smith's novel *Winter*, I felt robbed. After commencing as an ensemble of interesting, believable people, its characters became mouthpieces for ecology, nuclear plants, immigrants, working-class wages, horrors of Trumpian politics, and so forth. Story became wobbly and dangling as a baby tooth about to fall out. In the review I had to suggest that the book was mainly a "billboard" for Smith's (completely righteous) concerns.

(A piquant afterward is that *Winter* was soon thereafter shortlisted for the Orwell Prize for Political Writing—a prize most often given for nonfiction works.)

Political writing is a distinguished field, claiming a long line of notable practitioners. But literary fiction has a different goal, a different burden, and, above all, crucially different means for capturing our imaginations and accomplishing its work. And the (ironic) magic of literary writing is that it may be able to convey ideals far more powerfully than any billboarding.

Why? Because story, with its imperfection and eccentricity, assimilates inside us almost physically as well as psychically: slowly informing body and mind; continuing to dwell in us in ways that tracts—however eloquent—seldom can.

The infomercial reflex is not always crisply defined. Material can smear from Story into Advocacy and back again. You can look at a page and almost see a *Paid Political Announcement* disclaimer flashing like subtitles below the translucent prose. Some works veer membrane-close to becoming advertisements, or docudramas. Story may regain control and lose it again, in a kind of seesaw. Occasionally, Story finally "wins." I'm thinking now of Roxana Robinson's powerful novel *Cost*, which described a good family's near-destruction in its efforts to pay for the rehab of its youngest son, a heroin addict. In the course of this novel we learn a great deal about heroin addiction—but to the tremendous credit of Robinson's writing skills, Story won out.

Again: my argument is never with Cause. It's with the accelerating problem of Cause preempting the integrity, weight, and fluid primacy of art, or Story. And I remind you once more that this inversion is not always a bright, clean, obvious one.

It's easy to get into arguments about shades of gray: about who succeeded at making art without letting Cause tip or muddy that art—and who did not, and to what degree either way. Consider Kundera's *The Unbearable Lightness of Being*, which unfurled against the backdrop of the Prague Spring of 1968 through the invasion of Czechoslovakia by the Soviet Union. Story trumped everything in that work to me, or at least it did at the time I read it. Others may disagree.

Very much—maybe everything—depends upon who is reading, and when. Who is the Arbiter, or Observer? Who is defining? Who is curating?

Latina and gay; Black and experimental; Vietnamese and trans: any combination of background and vision, any hierarchy of ideals, you may argue, will want what it wants.

I stand by my original premise: Whatever the vision, it must be embedded at the molecular level, within and by and for the story form.

Otherwise, essentially, it's campaigning.

And it strikes me that these discussions, if never easily resolved, are more important to a democratic society than ever. Because the loss to us when art gets crushed by agenda spells a closing-off of one of the most vital human freedoms we know.

The hardest part? Discerning and assessing.

One measure of assessing the Storyness of a story is gut instinct: internal radar. If, in your reading ear, Op-Ed seems to have wrested the microphone from Story, it probably has. Proceed with caution. You could be wading into the smelly swamp of Sales Pitch. Because, relative to art, that's often what editorializing tends to be.

And I want to offer one more analogy now: a pretty straightforward one.

Literary art is still a contract in which the reader agrees to look at the proffered dream. If all goes well, we'll sign that contract eagerly, because we trust the voice of the dream. We'll take the dream inside our bodies (hearts, souls), let it time-release there—and be changed or nourished or haunted or hounded by it, subtly or dramatically, for the rest of our days.

That dream promises a truth—bound to no lobbyist or Cause but rather to the artist's vision of the universe at its marrow—the macro and micro of human life on earth. Katherine Anne Porter once described one of her stories as "a moral and emotional collision with a human situation." Each of those descriptions seems a fine thumbnail précis of the potential substance, freight, and momentum of literary work.

Art also agrees, in that contract, to teach us its own terms—how to read and understand it. Most artists (in most media) tell us pretty much straight off, *Here is the way I'm going to convey things to you, sometimes by indirection, in this particular language.*

In fact, this element—the *how* of its being, of its vision—provides one of art's most consistently powerful pleasures.

Even if we hardly remember particulars of books we've read that once meant everything to us, we still carry some part of them within us—if finally only a feeling they gave. That's not nothing. At some level they continue to shape and drive us, to inform how we act and think and feel. In this way, art survives and prevails, apart from sheer topicality.

I believe this is what art can do—what it *wants* to do.

Remember the old warning to writing students, about sending a telegram? Message with a capital M is not what a reader seeks. In fact, I believe an attentive reader can "smell" an incipient message or agenda in prose: This makes the material wilt and fade before her eyes. It makes her wary. She longs for Story to resume. If proselytizing takes over, the reader (recognizing it) may simply quit or reduce caring—rescinding belief. And belief's the ballgame. If the product morphs into a commercial, we're likely to treat it that way. The sense of being asked to swallow medicine has overtaken us. Such medicine may be very good for us. That can't change the fact that it's medicine.

Thus, readers paying close attention may feel like that vexed toddler in his highchair in the fabulous old *New Yorker* cartoon.

Its caption was written, legend has it, by the late, brilliant E. B. White. A little kid looks angrily from his bowl (of some dark scribbly mess) back to his parents. His face is screwed up with rage. He is onto their subterfuge. And he has no intention of buying it:

"I say it's spinach," he says. "And I say to hell with it!"

A reader likewise says to a blinkered work, "You stopped being a story and you became polemic. Whatever your good intentions, you've lost my trust."

We readers sometimes sense it coming before even opening a book: the publisher, or its blurbers, trumpet the work's significance in reverent tones.

O alas: beware reverence.

Now, let's talk about antidotes.

First, we need to employ vigilance and honesty in reading. Call it the Emperor's New Clothes reflex. We need to call out infomercialism where we find it. Slipping into boosterism contaminates art's integrity. Warning: This kind of calling-out won't make lots of friends. To state calmly and clearly that a work's Cause may be ultra-righteous but hijacks the work, won't go down well when that Cause is popular. And almost all of them are.

Second, as artists, we need to use the same vigilance and honesty in making our own work. By this I mean staying faithful to the story-making, its complex integrity; ensuring our work remains Story-centric. *Recover the direct gaze of a child.* Story must remain the god that all other elements serve.

In theory, we do this already. We undertook the writing life to do it.

Trust the micro to open out into the macro. Complexity supersedes Cause.

Art needs to be free. And so do we.

Another Art

Two or three minutes ago I was a smart, opinionated, recklessly healthy thirty-something, brooding about how few single, heterosexual men were left in San Francisco. Concurrent thoughts involved where any next social gathering might be, and how to get through Sundays.

A lonely bachelorette, I ate and drank anything. Sometimes I drank too much, soothing myself over the last crashed romance. I'd jog off the booze the next day at Golden Gate Park, then resume the cycles. Schmooze, brood, self-medicate. Repeat.

Nothing would ever change, since I was going to live forever.

I'd been *born* immortal, by the way. Just like my friends. We tried to carry the knowledge modestly. In my mind and the minds of my friends, we'd all simply sprung into the world fully formed like mythological gods: young, smart, good-looking, and—actually, yes— immortal.

It was honestly, in the words of Martin Amis, too bad about the others.

Some of those others had also had the unfortunate luck, it appeared, of being born old.

Well, it took all kinds, didn't it? And we, the young, pretty ones, could easily find or fake the generosity to jolly those luckless oldsters along. Our stores of energy were rich, self-replenishing. We could cheerfully shake the old folks' hands (only a tiny bit appalled by their soft grips, mottled skin, delicate bones, faintly unfamiliar smell). We could muster the polite wits to chat with them, ask how they were getting on. We found ways to appear interested in their answers. We stuck it out to listen—even if the answers bored us—controlling the urge to bolt.

Silently, we were relegating the oldsters' thinking and experience and spoken words to the Irrelevant pile.

I'm not proud of this.

It gets worse.

We secretly reckoned the old people's invisibility, their physical frailty, to be *their own fault*. That's correct, their fault. Falling apart meant, to us, loss of will. Loss of control felt easy to connect (in our demented thinking) to an abrupt disappearance of moral fiber, like succumbing to drug addiction or gaining morbid amounts of weight. Staying youthful and vigorous, by our reckoning, fell naturally into the category of a lifestyle choice—in point of fact, a *moral* choice. Fueling that astonishing belief was a constant current of pure, youthful cruelty—shocking, flip, heedless; perhaps ancient, perhaps animal-driven, the way herds would leave aging or infirm members behind.

Of course, that debate—about how much we can affect what we become, how much body follows mind—never ends. But try, as a quiet experiment, to catch your own silent judgments of various others, any hour of any day. How quickly, often how ruthlessly, we assume what we assume.

―――――

Thus, creeping decrepitude was, by our lights, ultimately their own doing—the elders' dullness, their bodily weaknesses or failures. They'd dropped the reins, fallen asleep at the wheel, given up. We'd do our best to forgive, and to humor them.

Meantime, my friends and lovers and I—well, we pretty much ran the world. We were gifted and beautiful, endearingly quirky, flamboyant—bursting with potential. Handily, the world seemed to have agreed to become as condensed and sparkling as we needed it to be—like a solitaire diamond we extended our hands to admire, turning it this way and that in the light.

We had forever, don't forget. Also, don't forget, we presented brilliantly: extremely easy on the eye. This alone excused and justified everything else.

Then, of course, like Hemingway's definition of going broke—slowly at first and then very, very fast—a series of seismic shifts occurred.

My gorgeous besties began to marry and have kids. In a reversal of the Ark story, two by two they left the expensive city—lighting out in a rhythmic diaspora for other territories. Eventually they posted photos and newsletters on social media. Their kids were adorable, clever, exhausting.

Five minutes later, those kids were graduating high school. Thirty seconds after that, they'd finished college. These kids of our friends, tall and sunburnt, joined the military, took jobs, and began to post their own photos from diverse domiciles: South America, Italy, Monterey, London, the Grand Canyon, Times Square—and soon enough, from hospital birthing rooms.

Agog, I beheld my besties cradling a scrinch-faced, bread-loaf-sized grandchild, sometimes crowned with feathery hair and eyebrows to match. And then another.

Then by default, I became one of them. My husband's son and his beautiful wife produced two perfect little girls, two years apart. *Howdy*, my husband croaked as they (twice) placed a rosebud of a scowling infant, her tiny fists clenched as if to punch someone, into his arms.

In three minutes, those baby girls grew into dazzling women. I am watching the second hand twitch along on any analog clock for their own adult-milestone reports. Meantime, my nieces and nephews, now tipping toward forty, have become wry, weary, still-somehow-good-looking parents to jewel babies of their own.

For God's sake—someone please stop this movie.

Those had been the *little kids*, those handsome parents—smiling, wise, baby-making, beer-quaffing. I'd held them and changed their diapers. They'd *been the little kids*. Moments ago. And then their *kids* became the kids—at least, for a few more moments. My sagging heart knows it's a matter of fractions of seconds before I'll glimpse birthing room shots from our most recent way-littles, who're in the process of instantly becoming Bigs.

How did I miss what I missed?

Ah, but this movie stops for no one.

I gaze at the grandparents—my own, immortal besties—in their online photos. They seem to have grown thinner, more brittle. Or they've become puffy and doughy under loose shirts, their faces taut, hair silver or gray, or gone. I stare and stare at them.

I stare at myself. (Who loves seeing their own cross-hatched face on Facetime or Zoom among my peers? No one. None of us. One comedian quipped that if he sees himself naked in the mirror now he wants to "shoot at himself and run back to the car.")

————

What happens next is the no-magic-wand-available part.

I've made up all the names. The people are real.

In a roll call of my peers: Calvin has a fibrillating heart. After umpteen procedures, he's seeming okay—for now. Raymond's grown huge, eating and drinking whatever he wants after a diagnosis of stomach cancer, but somehow not yet perishing of it. Gene collapsed at his job one day, skinny as a stick but suffering from high blood pressure. Barry walks with a cane because his morbid weight vexes his knees and ankles. Fred, who lives alone, has begun saying the same things over and over. He forgets what you've just told him. His son has just settled him into assisted care.

We've lost Stephen. Renal failure. Marvin's gone now, too: lungs, I think, though it may have begun as prostate. Pancreatic is taking Kenny. He held it off a good while, but now it's having its way.

The women parallel all this. Breasts, ovaries, brains. Zero rhyme or reason.

These are the exigencies. No one "willed" it.

I try to avoid following the obits.

We survivors—slow to comprehend this monumental shift—do

admit to owning a menu of our own minor humbugs. It takes longer to bounce back from colds and viruses. Energy wanes. Sleep's elusive. Muscle and bone rebel by turns, with no traceable cause. Sudden itches or stabs of pain or swamp-bog malaises erupt, absolutely unexplainable. References like "bursitis" and "hip replacement" and "new knee" become commonplace, not to mention, let us say, digestive challenges.

Remembering is harder. Driving at night's no fun. Everything one puts in one's mouth, one immediately wears. And feels.

Most of us are on statins. We know how to read lab results.

Weirdest of all? People have begun to look through us or past us. *Us!*

We who'd always owned the scene, created the action—we, the future's hope—we who turned heads; the sexy, spunky, radiant royalty in the room.

It seemed to happen, I insist, slowly at first. Then very, very fast.

———

I am now the same age as Bonnie Raitt, Meryl Streep—and yes, Martin Amis. Knock on wood—oh, *hug* wood, *kiss* wood—I am still strong, clear-minded, fruitful.

But I have a friend who is thirteen years older than I am, who lives on the other side of the country. She is a widow: a warm, gifted, articulate writer. Her several grown children visit her often. I admired a book of hers years ago, wrote a fan letter. We've been e–pen pals ever since.

I hear less from her lately—this lively, creative, curious, modest, sturdy, uncomplaining, astute being who works out at the gym, reads deeply, and (until the pandemic) made regular pilgrimages to different cities to take in theater and art. She worries about all the same bodily vexations described above. She also worries that she and her (ninety-something) boyfriend are "losing intellectual ground." Their friends are starting to die, or suffer incapacitation, faster.

I tell my husband about my friend.

(My husband's a sane, steady man who braved odds, back during my bachelorette days, to drive the hour south to San Francisco for a fateful blind date with me.)

He looks at me calmly. He's already lost his parents, and many friends. He shrugs: "It's all going in one direction."

He has come to perceive, he tells me, that when we are young we project ourselves into time. Now, he suggests, time is *coming at us* point-blank, at rampaging speed. Our mission at this hour? To slow it down—but also, sensibly enough, to enjoy it.

Be clear: pain and loss are not the only door prizes of aging. And contrary to popular thought, older people don't spend most of their time hanging out in timorous clusters glancing at the sky every five minutes to make sure nothing's falling. The sweetnesses arriving to aging people can be very many, and here in no particular order are a few:

All the arts. Nature. Food and drink. Health and friendship. Adored family.

Beauty. Heroism. Wonder.

Yes, and sex.

Realer than real, all these, if we're lucky. Steadily so. The final stanza in a Tony Hoagland poem, which I love, states:

I have news for you—
there are people who get up in the morning and cross a room

and open a window to let the sweet breeze in
and let it touch them all over their faces and bodies.

Coming full circle: when we're young, the annoyance of aging seems a far, far country. We avoid thinking about it for fear it may infect us by sheer association. Then, too quickly, our parents have moved there—first with wit, equanimity, even zest. Inevitably, the people who gave us life begin to falter, and one abrupt day, they vanish.

Then, somehow, we and our friends find ourselves stepping across that far country's borders, being waved (impatiently) through customs.

Something smells odd.

In other words: I'm catching up with my pen pal.

As Wendy explains, years later, to a revisiting Peter Pan, who is straight-up horrified to see that despite their vows she has allowed herself to grow up: *I couldn't help it, Peter.*

I couldn't help it. *We* couldn't help it.

And bound up in that terrible confrontation, I think—bound up in Peter's shock and dismay, and Wendy's abject haplessness—is an entire generation's sturdy assumption (weaned on Disney animation and Disney morals after the Second World War), that if we behaved well and tried to do good, good would naturally flow back to us; that as a kind of bonus, we'd never age, or die.

———

I sat the other morning in the warming sun with my coffee, peering up into the fluffy green Japanese maple that shades our backyard, a tree beloved to me, surely at least as old as me, home to generations of finches, jays, robins—robins who hold parties there every spring, drunk on purple-black privet berries and swooping recklessly, cackling.

In fall those green leaves turn the colors of fire opals.

Sometimes my husband and I conduct little mock arguments about which season we love best. We end up sheepish, admitting we love them all for different reasons—the way you love each child in your life for different reasons (sidelining all cracks about climate change).

That morning, thinking about the merry-go-round of seasons and how unwilling I'd be to sacrifice any of them, I began to understand somewhere behind my ribcage that the amount of time between my older friend's realities and my own has shrunk. Her shocks and setbacks no longer seem exotic, like random bad luck or inscrutable fallout from lapsed will. I remembered a Richard Wilbur poem whose title alone is a poem: "Love Calls Us to the Things of This World." I understood that I need to make, for my friend and for myself, a small effort of imagination that may surely be called love— the kind of love I know I will crave when the same soul-crushing trials close in on me.

A small effort of imagination, late in the season.

A couple of other poems may apply here.

"*The art of losing isn't hard to master*," wrote Elizabeth Bishop. "*No man is an island*," wrote John Donne, a line once memorized by schoolchildren. Loss may be one definition of living. There are others. "*Every man is a piece of the continent*," added Donne, "*a part of the main.*" At our best, as a species, many of us still flock to steady the one who falters. I've seen it happen; it happens all the time. But that reflex feels more urgent now—a gentle caution as well as a mandate.

A matter of the heart, taking a walk.

What might it look like, this late awareness? What form might it take? Borrowing the great, abiding question of art: How, then, shall we live?

I sense that good answers are invented in situ, case by case—holding tightly to that single mantra known as the oldest of measures, the Golden Rule.

What will *I* want? What might *you* want? How does *anyone* long to be treated at age two or at a hundred and two?

I would hope, first, to be heard. *Attention must be paid.* So, one listens—with care, compassion—deploying the above small act of imagination.

Next, I would like to be perceived as viable. Alive. Possibility persists in the breathing organism. Mystery and possibility still dwell and evolve in a living being *whose story is not over.* Forget actuarial numbers. What matters is the human before you containing heaven knows what extraordinary history and gifts—and still, somehow, yes, a future.

One listens. One sees. One takes in the story. One lets the story enter the heart. One accomplishes all this in real time—with patience and without thinking, *Wow, what a special person I am for doing this*. If real interest and affection can flavor these transactions, superb. If they cannot? *Respect* manages it. Respect for the quiet, daily heroism: for the expressed resolve.

Let's carry on. Let's talk again. Do you need anything?

The other art.

Your Baby's Ugly

I once asked an admired, awarded, serious literary writer who's something of a Name, of some gravitas in the writing world—yet a kind and generous friend to me—how she was feeling following an ambitious (pre-pandemic) book tour.

"Fragile" was her answer.

That response puzzled me.

It struck me as a bit self-indulgent, even petulant. After all, the hard bottom line is that most writers would kill to encounter the "problem" of book-tour fatigue. In a best case it means a publisher believed in your work enough to fund the tour. More commonly, you had to fund it yourself—but that meant you'd be even more motivated to make it count. If we throw our souls into getting work accepted for publication, it follows we must next throw our souls into creating buzz for the product. True, each phase of this requires Herculean stores of drive, energy, stamina, and also—trickier for introverted writers—a willingness to wade into clusters of people, both in person and remotely, and behave pleasantly enough to encourage their interest. Book tours for a major publisher, of the sort my friend endured, have routinely been defined as ultra-demanding.

But surely (I told myself again after she confessed) tour fatigue was a luxurious problem: a bona fide spoil of the long struggle.

In other words? Suck it up, Major Writer. Do your duty.

But after a visit to a book group some while back (also pre-virus), I was forced to reconsider my flip stance. What anyone outside the process might presume to be a joyful task—not to say honor and privilege—turned out to be, well, not so much.

I'd assumed until then that talking to book groups guaranteed a lovefest.

An author visiting a reading group could feel, I figured, pre-vetted. A bunch of individuals had read your book, agreed it was worth pursuing, and invited you to visit and talk about it. To my mind that meant they'd liked it enough to want to learn more.

Maybe most of the time, that's still what happens. An author sits down (if on-screen now) among a collection of friendly faces and, prompted by their eager questions, thinks out loud to them about the making of the book, her writing path, and whatever funny or sad or silly anecdotes she can link up for their entertainment.

This last round, pre-pandemic, I drove to a gathering of intelligent, affluent women in a beautiful, woodsy setting—one of those houses built by its progressive, artful owners. Everybody was well educated, fit, confident. They'd all read the book (a positive sign), and several of them cornered me at once to sign their copies. So far, so good.

But after we'd seated ourselves in the cozy, sunken living room, and a couple of members had made nice noises about enjoying the novel, I noticed several others sitting with tight mouths and folded arms, eyeing me narrowly.

One of this latter faction remarked, as her opening salvo, that she did not believe my characters' ages. At fifty-eight and sixty-two, they weren't old enough, she felt, to consider themselves to be aging.

She herself was fifty-something.

I stared at her. True: I'd made those two main characters a little younger than they should technically have been. Nobody wants to read about super-old people. I blinked like a raccoon in flashlight beams, trying to think of a way to say this.

But before I could, another member suddenly declared that those same two protagonists, old friends who irritate each other and finally erupt into a climactic whopper of a fight, *did not really love one another.*

This completely blindsided me.

Was I expected to *argue*?

A third member then cocked her head. "How did you come to write in so many sentence fragments?" she demanded, in a tone striving for clinical curiosity—which only underscored her obvious, sharp dislike of sentence fragments.

Slowly, I explained that I was closely tracking the interior thoughts of these characters, and that to my knowledge people didn't tend to think in structured, grammatically complete sentences—rather, thoughts came in clumps of words with abrupt starts and stops. Often, I added, certain words and phrases referred to personal history, which then functioned as a kind of shorthand.

This explanation met polite silence. I'd thrown a pebble down a bottomless well. My stomach started to sort of squinch. I put my little plate of olives aside.

As for characters not loving each other? I opened my hands: "That's up to you," I said as cheerfully as I could. Those characters *belong to you now*, I reminded them—trying to echo Elizabeth Strout's brilliant response when listeners buttonholed her about who the model may have been for Strout's fabulous protagonist, Olive Kitteridge. I reasoned that if I dared contradict these women's convictions about who loved whom, or about characters not acting their ages, they would simply turn on me and tell me I was wrong: dead wrong.

The women laughed uneasily when I suggested the above to them, recognizing (I hoped) at least some of the built-in absurdity of our impasse.

We stumbled on. I could not allow myself more than a single beer, since I knew I had to drive. And though on the face of it people were civil, by the end of the night I was feeling, well—emptied. Unpersuasive. And somewhat brutalized, like a witness on the stand whose alibi is considered fishy. I couldn't wait to flee home, get a stiff drink down, and talk it over with my husband.

A college teacher who's spoken all his life before roomfuls of individuals, he reminded me (as I stared at my margarita) that people bring unknowable baggage to their readings—and to the author. You simply can't, he said, second-guess what backstories will shape their responses—why one or another seems to be watching you with suspicion, scorn, even rage. No rating sheet's handed back to authors—except in the form of unpredictable behavior. No follow-up evaluation notes appear—unless you count book sales.

Alas. Much of the time that's exactly what counts, and what is measured: sales. Never mind what a book cost its maker at any level, figurative or literal, to create or promote. Readers style themselves as consumers, wielding a personal manifesto of consumer rights. They expect a warrantied level of satisfaction. If that feels missing to them, its absence will be announced—by word of mouth or a bad online review, or both—or as a sour face and an accusatory questioning during book-group visits or bookstore readings. (For a horrifying account of "Amazon's commodification of fiction" into a vast shatter-belt of ultra-customized, on-demand genres, see Parul Sehgal's "All You Can Read" in the *New Yorker*.)

I confess here to writing a species of literary fiction that's urgently interior and cerebral. I'm not ashamed of this, because that also happens to be the kind of work I like to read. But I still burn, remembering the evening an audience member took me to task for it during a packed bookstore launch of an earlier story collection.

She raised her hand and asked calmly, "Do you read newspapers?"

I gaped at her.

She repeated the question. I'd understood her the first time, but I'd felt so amazed by this poison-tipped arrow of a tactic that it took me a couple of beats to shape a response. The woman was suggesting, fairly bitterly, that the work I made paid no attention to the *real* news: that my stories were hopelessly interior, self-immersed, oblivious of what was truly important in the world—therefore irrelevant.

Plenty of criticism of this nature has been aimed at writers like me—also at certain writers in prior eras; for example, Jane Austen. (I don't wish to suggest my work compares with hers, but to offer a broad parallel.)

I am still trying to understand my feelings about such moments, because I'm supposed to be a seasoned pro. I've been writing for over thirty years. I've spoken to classes, bookstore audiences, reading groups. I'm supposed to have learned to steel myself against *that look*—the wary eyeballing—and to bounce back from it.

Yet the group in the arty woodland retreat, for all its surface courtesy and pleasant food and rural chic, reminded me I'm still as vulnerable as any newbie—prey to feeling attacked, misread, or just plain ignored, relegated to scenery.

Granted: A writer tends by definition to have no skin. She is hopelessly, some say ruinously, sensitive to the subtlest nuances of atmosphere, language, behavior—but especially language. How to defend this, after twelve books? *Nolo contendere.* I should be tougher. Cagier. Cannier. You put your art into the world: you take your lumps. People have crazy stuff to work out. You shut up. You carry on.

But it's hard out there for the skinless. Being flung onto the defensive for my work made me feel like I'd eaten something that had gone bad. Worse, I felt lonelier. Most of those people seemed not at all to *get* the novel's vision; its passion, its quest. They seemed instead to want to pick quarrels with tiny particulars—as though my "correcting" said particulars would fix some larger, overall problem. They seemed never to grasp or take to heart the story's raw thrust, its vibrancy, the "force through its green fuse," to swipe a famous phrase.

But how can an author hit a reader in the heart, if not through her work?

Debating skills won't cut it.

Some authors might shrug here: "not my circus." Others may slump and nod sadly: the art has failed. But that can't make sense if a majority of readers loved the same work.

Which, thank the freaking stars, they did.

One thing's sure: Self-castigation won't fix this. Nor can it make more art.

So I've pondered how to retool—how to carry on after confrontations like these (because there'll be more). How to replenish and protect what is needed for carrying on: vigor, urgency, fearlessness. Freedom. Confidence to make a mess, to spatter.

It's one thing to consider a notion of hostile readers in the abstract: say, as a dim clump of grumbling citizens (in my mind they're mud-streaked and dressed in gray rags like *Les Miserables* revolutionaries), milling around resentfully at the horizon. You can read the terrible reviews they write on Amazon and elsewhere: often crude, cranky, sometimes misspelled.

It's another thing to be eating their pasta salad, petting their cat, and gazing into their vexed faces as they insist you explain why you did something they do not like.

I'd like to have answered them more simply.

I made this book and I'm proud of it, but its life is its own now. You can like it or hate it. I can't be required to defend or justify it.

Except no one really believes that. Maybe not even me. I laid down those damned sentences, didn't I?

Nonetheless: Statements like the italics above should probably be printed in the front matter of any new book. They can serve as a generic caution, a standard-issue, no-comment comment alongside the usual disclaimers meant to deflect lawsuits: "These characters are purely fictional," and so on. I've always believed that the moment an author tries to defend or justify her work she is *tacitly validating her accuser's objection*, like trying to form a response to *Have you stopped beating your wife yet?*

Meantime the author-as-mortal faces, as noted above, a different kind of loneliness. Loneliness, of course, is nothing new to writers; it's a preexisting, often chosen condition. We go off by ourselves as a rule. Solitude is treasure.

This new loneliness, however, springs from—let us say—a rather rude reception.

Roughly translated? *Your baby's ugly.*

Hearing this, a writer's brain circles the world in three seconds, resuming at square one.

You want people to read, and to love reading.

You bang your gong to bring attention to the hard-wrought book.

Then? Gird yourself, earnest artist. When attention comes it will contain naysayers.

There will always be people who'll love your work—and almost unfailingly, those who won't: a fringe gang of thumbs-downers with rather bafflingly specific agendas. The writer must allow for this, even prepare for it—must learn to grow some temporary skin or, at very least, place herself at psychic distance.

She cannot feel obliged to solve it. Humans are too various.

Above all: she must never, never, never let it puncture or stall or tarnish or poison or even shade her ownership of, faith in, and energy for her work.

I recently watched a PBS feature on the life of conductor Michael Tilson Thomas, seventy-five years old at the time of its airing. In it, MTT described a moment when, as a very young, up-and-coming conductor, he had politely asked the mighty Leonard Bernstein what Bernstein had thought of MTT's just-completed performance of a difficult orchestral work.

Maestro Bernstein answered—here I paraphrase—"One you take possession of it and truly make it your own, you won't need to care what I or anybody else thinks of it."

Fragile, me? Yeah, so it seems. I could spend time regretting it— but I no longer have that kind of time. And I can't recommend regret as a fruitful way for anyone to use what time remains.

So just here, friends, arrives the saving upside: Skinlessness and vulnerability must *qualify as another tool in the toolbox*, part of an author's catchment system, her intake radar—the hypersensitive, hyper-porous apparatus that locates, gathers, and sifts incoming materials. From these, eventually, she makes new work. I am doing it here, writing about the blunt trauma of being dissed by a book group. How can I want to retract or eradicate a necessary tool? A best friend used to enjoy (fondly) calling me *a pulpy mess*. I couldn't argue with her. An excruciating awareness conferred in childhood, something never grown out of—chronic, unrefined—turns out also to be something I *happen to need*.

Bruised? A little. But bruises go away. I notice them for a while with a kind of morbid fascination, the way we all do. I may write about them. Then after a time, like the rest of us, I turn to other projects.

By then, everything else has become so much more interesting.

The Lonely Voice in Its Bathrobe: A Life of Letters

"Words are events, they do things, change things. They transform both speaker and hearer; they feed energy back and forth and amplify it. They feed understanding or emotion back and forth, and amplify it."

—URSULA LEGUIN

"There is something about the very form and occasion of a letter—the possibility it offers, the chance to be as open and tentative and uncertain as one likes and also the chance to formulate certain ideas, very precisely—if one is lucky in one's thoughts."

—JAMES WRIGHT

What *is* it, finally, about letters? Why does this old-fashioned form, even maimed and shrunken, volleyed mostly through the ether now by countless devices, still squinch our chests to receive it—the way a wrapped gift makes us draw extra breath? Why can letters stop us, sidetrack us—anywhere, anytime—to command attention? Why are they irresistible?

To me—no exaggeration—letters are everything.

They pierce to the bone, the heart. They flirt. They agonize. They risk, wallow, forge.

They noodle. Galvanize. Grieve. Oh, do they grieve.

But they also revel, and reveal. They give something. Many somethings.

I give them nearly everything.

Yet during Late Work years—speaking for myself—my hemorrhaging love for letters has been, say, tourniqueted. Meaning I still obsess madly while making them; polish them to the inmost grain. But once they're sent, I coldly destroy them.

All of them. My own, and those from others.

Is that strange? Read on.

In thinking about letters we must first discount the confetti—the empty noise; the formality, obfuscation, politics, social blather—also those proposing blackmail, bribery, or hookups. Ransom notes, position papers, embossed cards *from the desk of.* Clever announcements, newsletters, bread and butter: out. Also—alas—suicide notes.

The above can't obtain for this focus. (If someone makes art of them, bravo, but that will deserve a separate study.)

The kind I cherish (and pour nonstop into the ethersphere) are the ad hoc, bald, raw, state-of-the-state *booms*: what Dorothy Parker called "a burst of the frankies." Parker was talking about those spontaneous, artless blurts uttered aloud in company, often at drinks or dinner—often colorfully offensive.

For the purpose of letters, "company" means my reader. And the spirit of the frankies is what I adore and crave. "If you haven't got anything nice to say, come sit by me," as Alice Roosevelt Longworth is said to have cracked. The feckless freedom of the letter-writing I love cares not a particle about offending. (Sender's Remorse, on the other hand, remains too real and tortures too many, myself at their forefront. *Should I have said that?* Dear God, the time spent.)

For me, the urgent letter-from-the-heart risks by definition—a more complex project than mere dinner-table antics—protected and nurtured as it is by time, space, reflection. The reader's attention to that letter likewise becomes a different animal: rapt, careful analysis. Of course I now refer mainly to email letters, since they've pretty much taken over the genre. Full disclosure: email consumes my days. I tend it like a garden. Often I lie awake trying to interpret or solve a confusion or injury received through an e-letter, or squander absurd amounts of time wording a response. Despite its evanescence, the form is dangerously potent. Most terrifyingly, it's unretractable: once sent, gone. Like Zorro's sword, it can leave bloody lacerations across the heart in a stroke. Even the subtlest shift in tone can launch rounds of agonized second-guessing. (*X sounds cold. What did I say?* See Sender's Remorse.) It may prove impossible to fix the damage, or to find an answer to real or imagined slights.

Heady and cathartic, e-letters also feel cheap as tissue because they're so instantly disposable. This changes their valence, for better and worse.

E-letters and similar message forms, including social-media posts, remain seductive to writers for a thousand reasons, starting with the very fact that while they cost only electricity they're still *written*. Deliciousness is compounded by the weightless ease of their making: their instant malleability; the overpowering freedom with which they're composed and remade. These conditions can actually get writers high. We're invisible, airborne, mobile. At total liberty to say anything and finesse it to a fine grain, even in plain sight—say, at a crowded café. Who wouldn't exult?

About letters, I carry—might it be obvious?—all the feelings.

Though rarely considered Art in the hour of their making, many letters become art. It only takes time. While they tend to reveal what a friend calls the "back of the weave" (dreary dailiness, ugly knots), certain letters live on. In their aftermath—often following a writer's death—someone proposes to collect and edit them for publication. Such collections may become fiercely personal to many, releasing precisely the needed insight when consulted, like the I Ching. Think of Rilke, Van Gogh, William Maxwell, Virginia Woolf; Louise Bogan; Flannery O'Connor; Elizabeth Bishop to Robert Lowell; Leslie Marmon Silko to James Wright; Wright's own *Collected Letters* to fellow poets like Donald Hall, Theodore Roethke, Galway Kinnell, James Dickey, Mary Oliver, Robert Bly.

Sometimes it's the letters' very dailiness, their homeliness, that pierces us: illness, birth and death and disasters (Bogan's house burned down), money, love, legal humbug, travel, work, weather. At others it's the raw, unrefined yearning—often written (blurted) during a writer's or an artist's youth. We recognize ourselves—sometimes with alarm—mainly relieved we're not so odd or even, perhaps, so cursed. The range of preoccupations proves large. Van Gogh worried to his beloved brother Theo about sales of his works; about costs of food and supplies. Mary McCarthy told Hannah Arendt it might be best to take her tea in her hotel room and coffee later in the lobby. Silko's musings include time and energy expended in working with students ("It's only sometimes I get lonesome for my own work"), about her mares having foaled, about a grandmother's broken hip.

We savor epistolary literature like *Charing Cross Road* or *Meet Me at the Museum*—at least I do. Alice Munro's immortal collection *Carried Away* begins with a brief exchange of letters that quietly slices off the top of your head. The era, the author's notoriety (often assigned much later), the cultural moment during which the letters were written, the cultural moment of considering them—all these define the letters' value over time, their necessity; their greatness.

Dozens of analogies for what letters can mean shimmer forward. I think of opalescent shells washing musically ashore. Real lives were lived inside each one—untold, *until* we examine the shell and begin to surmise from its shape and quality what its occupant's existence might have been. The shell—the letter—lives on. (No one's yet solved the terrible question of preserving e-letters, which mostly disappear.) Paper letters may now in fact be considered the old-fashioned pearls of prior, lived lives, however fragile—an expressed, timeless product of compression and ordeal.

There are people to whom I have written all my life, whom I'll be writing till the last. That alone fairly amazes me. What other tie (besides family, partner, or art itself) commands such loyalty? Making letters has always felt—since I can remember—desperately, joyfully important. Why?

Here Is the Church, Here Is the Steeple

One writes letters in two directions: to the self, and to another. (The term *The Other* holds problematic connotations.) One reaches out to a fellow creature so one might be witnessed, and not pass from this earth unremarked. Like floating a bottled message out to sea, the gesture implies faith and trust that a caring recipient will gesture back—will participate by absorbing and responding. (Nothing wallops me like the sight, in books or films, of a pile of unopened, unread letters.) True: letters can bode badly; can try reader and writer alike if they involve terrible news or other pain. But they can also supply new energy, recognition, joy. Visual artists have made memorable use of the telling moment of reading a physical letter. Recall two exquisite Vermeers: *The Letter Reader* and *Girl Reading a Letter at an Open Window*. Gazing at those paintings stops time, giving us the voluptuous, suspended moment of that particular bliss.

The companion impulse of letter-writing may be that of adding to a formalized journal—a more structured way of talking to oneself because it organizes itself to speak to a sympathetic witness, thus inducing a different consciousness. Yiyun Li calls a diary "a letter to oneself." (She also laments how traditional diaries and letters are disappearing from contemporary life.) Letters to *other* than oneself are by comparison distinguished by the awareness of addressing that separate pair of eyes, obliging a writer to organize and clarify in ways not strictly necessary when writing to oneself. *This happened, then that; here's how; here's the way I feel.* One's conveying experience—never entirely, but earnestly—to Another.

Thus the energy of letters (*I am; you are; here is the church; here is the steeple*) travels in two directions: the first enters the perception of the reader, while the second loops straight back (both during composing and rereading) into the writer's heart, distilling her thinking but also making it larger. Letters recapitulate our confinement in flesh, but also our spiritual and intellectual travel. In all cases, selfness receives new blood in the telling. That strikes me as a species of miracle. Reality's made more real when the writer knows Another will be building it afresh in their mind and heart.

A letter's a made thing. That's its Art potential. Even if we throw letters away nine hundred times an hour—which we so much, so easily do. Killing darlings right and left.

All those letters! Each requires energy, brainpower, time. Lots of writers insist letters are a waste of time, of clearest energy. A rabbit hole. Yet it's one I tumble down gladly, deliberately, daily—as if into an illicit affair or drug.

I cannot wait, each day, to square off with letters. Writing them comforts, braces, clarifies. They force me to *muster*—like dowsing for thoughts not yet known—but also to please myself. As the Brits say: one gets things sorted; one sorts oneself out. This removes a big chunk of terror out of facing the real work later, because it will feel more like a simple extension—like a relative—of letter-writing. Making letters prior to facing real work feels like stretching before running: arms, hands, and mind flexing; lungs filling; starting to roll. I remember Anne Lamott's edict that a writer should keep herself in delight. The late Jessica Mitford claimed she wrote letters first thing each day simply to warm up for pending work.

That's some distinguished precedent.

But honestly? I relish making them: the zero-gravity somersaults, the featherweight, zip-zap rebounds—the sharp, clean air of a pristine horizon. I suppose this makes it sound like flying. It sort of is. Just *anticipating* letter-writing is erotic for me—the way approaching a bloc of private writing time and space is erotic.

Why? For the same reason my husband loves a sparklingly set dinner table almost more than he loves the meal that will follow: a universe of possibility glitters there, a portal. It's that liminal space, the hoped-for, not-yet-fully-imagined motions and substance that may next fill it, that enchants and sparks us. I'm *eager to find out what I think*. It's not known—but always about to begin to appear. I'll know more once I start. Thing will lead to thing. Thing will *wick forth* thing. Later I can work with whatever emerged. Later I'll better understand everything—the larger context, my own oblique purposes, unforeseen connections.

Edging toward a new comprehension's brink thrills almost more than revelation itself.

What's most erotic about making letters may involve an interim dream-self constructed while writing—partly wishful—inhabiting what the brilliant writer Andre Aciman calls the *irrealis* mode: a dimension neither past nor future but ever possible. It's a construct like a holograph, a separate-yet-parallel dimension hovering just at hand. In letters a writer shapes and smooths that construct infinitely, taking infinite pleasure in the *what-if*-ness moving toward *just-about-to*-ness. The being I want to be, all the shadings of mind and heart and soul I long to convey—to please myself; to impress another—these pump light into that turning, dimensional form. I fiddle with them continuously in letters—trying to describe, to perfect, that conflation.

Everything's Forgotten

Letter-writing's pleasures still smart around the edges for me with old guilt. Writers own, let's face it, a notorious capacity for punishing themselves. I remember reading one writer's vow that he *would not let himself out of his chair to get more coffee* because that meant postponing the true, hard thing going on inside the work. This struck me as almost a parody of self-torture. It reminds me how our fondness for suffering still gives us heartburn—how we still see the ancient myth of suffering as a true measure of art; the questing seeker passing through fire, blah, blah. Granted, I've used my own suffering for writing. And making art often feels bewildering; we're anxious, uncertain, and the freefall lostness of it can sicken or panic us—the stomach drops—like being unable to find one's car. But not always. And what's still and forever true is *everyone invents their own way* through nasty weather. (You get used to losing the car and just wander for a while pretending not to care, whistling in a way that fakes insouciance.) And making art—being alive, for that matter—is weather. Which passes (like everything else). It's only basic logic that one method or navigation trick can't be expected to work for everyone.

Making letters relieves me. As do the other kinds of writing. I do all of them.

Afterward, I delete the letters. Time can delete the articles and books.

This cheerful fatalism came late: a bona fide, Late Work windfall—born from an updated sense of what matters: very little, as it turns out, besides health, love, and art. I used to think, in something like the White Rabbit's alarm, *Oh my God, posterity.* I kept cartons of letters (typed, single-spaced, multipaged) and for some while, lugged them wherever I moved. A few years ago the California State Library offered to archive my papers. Elated for a luscious reason to shovel out the office, I sent a dozen boxes (manuscripts, notes, photocopies, mementos, letters) to that good entity. I'm pretty sure the material will eventually be digitized—*and* that almost no one will know or care.

That's fine.

Honest.

People juggle complicated lives until, as drily noted by writer Joan Acocella, "we throw up our hands and die." Everyone's racing inside their hamster wheel, until they can't. In my playwright husband's own merry words during an interview, "everything's forgotten!" If you dwell with this calm truth a while, it clears the table. There's forgiveness in it. There's a purifying fatalism in it. It also erases performance anxiety—whatever remains of that.

Thus, before I destroy letters I reread them—several times. Sometimes I pull them from the e-trash to read them several times more. Then I delete and forget them.

Obsessive, right?

The compulsive rereading instinct drives revision elsewhere, too. I need to confirm that the language and ideas, on review, hold their accuracy; that the music still plays. I need to sound out sentences in my head, let eyes and ears mull their shape and heft, marinate in their resonance. The overarching wish is for the work—the letter—to make its mark; to pulse even briefly inside its reader, stand about in there for a moment like little senators, nobly arguing.

Showing off? God, yes. I'd be lying to deny it.

Yet the enchantment with my own voice can crumble. As if poisoned I may seize up, sickened by my own plummy arrogance. It can begin to sound to me like the love child of Ray Bradbury with some fusty librarian—or worse: like someone who *wants you to think she is smart.* Though I often tell writers there's absolutely nothing left to fear and we'll all be dead soon, I notice myself going stiff with dread now and then: fearing I've seriously blown it, written something stupid or harsh or shallow, selfish or archaic. Yes, I want to sound smart. I also want to delight and surprise, reach into hearts. I want my reader to stop cold and think, *Oh, I know just what you mean*—to tingle with a rush of identification.

Yet I also know we'll both soon forget every last crumb of all of it. I've forgotten most everything. Why shouldn't everyone else?

The unthinkable *will* happen. We're all going there. Here is the church. Here is the steeple.

This, too, provides its own hamster wheel.

Dear Maria and Love, Joan

I began my writing life with letters. They opened the big, blocky—but, once opened, breeze-filled—door. I loved nothing better at the beginning than to sit and pound away at the Royal Portable typewriter (a gift from my late beloved dad, a professor who typed like a classical pianist on speed). It felt right—like distilled purpose. For more years than I can name I wrote long, dense, single-spaced letters to friends and family. Paraphrasing Robert Bly, the more I typed, the better I felt. I knew I was sublimating—knew I secretly longed to be doing "real writing." But for years I felt totally unqualified. I couldn't imagine I owned enough wisdom, which was what I thought was required.

Letters were all I had. In them, I felt whole, private, free.

Dear heaven, did they issue.

As a young woman exiled to a tiny town called Kolda in the Senegalese bush during a Peace Corps stint, I wrote thick bundles of pages by hand from the mud cabin where I lived, out near a river and a tangle of jungle. So many anguished pages. What I was really saying in all of them—besides describing exotic terrain, adding iodine to boiled water, spending hours squatting over a hole in the ground watching an enormous skyful of stars; the kind, wry Senegalese people who always tried to help me—besides reporting those impressions, I was of course saying *I am so sad and lonely I don't think I can keep doing this.* I was begging to be understood and (long, long shot) forgiven.

My failure to stick it out in Senegal remained, all my life, a source of terrible, secret shame. I returned home only months into the assignment. There I tried to gather myself, overmaster my shame, and start again. I was perhaps twenty-one.

The letters continued through umpteen lives. I moved to Hawaii and letters poured from the Royal Portable: to mainland friends, my dad, my high school English teacher, my sweet younger sister. Writing as a calling—a notion of making art—would not catch fire until many years later, long after my dear dad was dead. But when it did, the earth paused in its turning. Dabbling in journalism had helped. I date it from the thunderclap realization that if I simply cut off the greeting and closing lines from a completed letter—"Dear Maria" and "Love, Joan"—I had an essay before me. Essays led to short stories, which led to novels, then back to longer, more textured essays, then on to more novels, stories—and still more essays.

Twelve books later, the letters never stopped.

They continue to this hour.

The Lonely Voice in Its Bathrobe

A favorite image, one I love to replay in my head and tell others about, is that of the late, beloved author and editor William Maxwell, who famously insisted on going to each day's writing in his pajamas and robe straight from the breakfast table in the morning. No mystery there: it reassures and even demonstrates my own instincts. One needs to take the mind straight from that fertile, porous state just after sleep, still in soft, loose clothing, directly to the keyboard or notebook, whenever possible. Mysterious energy—residual dreams— may transmute to the work in ways no writer yet totally understands. Unbinding garments ease the work's flow through the body, letting them breathe together. Never mind about John Cheever putting on a suit and tie to take an elevator down to his building's basement, where he apparently sat all day in a writing office he maintained there. Ample room (for the deepest breath you can take) inside pajama softness lets the spirit roam.

But here's the delicious capper. Maxwell was also known to

demand (as his renown grew) that interviewers who insisted on visiting his home to question him face-to-face allow him to go to his typewriter and *type out his answers to their questions.*

Yes. Right there, while the interviewer waited silently across the room. Then he'd simply hand his questioner the paper he'd answered upon.

Don't you just fall out of your chair, loving this? Maxwell had to *find out what he thought* the best way he knew—unmuddied by voice noise or ego noise. A different voice spoke when thoughts were summoned, organized, typed out. I so passionately align with this method that I would *often rather write someone than see them in person.* Maxwell's adaptation brazenly enacts my own prejudice for writing letters—the sanctuary and nourishment they afford—over almost every other form of communication, including FaceTime and Zoom (unless maybe we're all drinking something fabulous).

In shame, I've had to admit to well-meaning friends that I hate the phone.

It's like admitting to carrying a distasteful disease. Dear *God* how I hate the phone. What happens on the phone? Nervousness. Social noise. Everyone scrambling to be polite; to move niceness around like a shuffleboard puck. Nothing raw or rich or substantive or complex gets said—unless one or both speakers have had a ton of practice or are loquaciously drunk, which often creates other problems.

A writer's introversion has everything to do with this.

Most of us can't wait to race home after being forced to interact somewhere—to work through what we think about what just happened and soothe ourselves into settling back down. Ruminating's not a valued currency out and about, in the best of times. To ruminate *uninterrupted* (a word that for many years was perhaps my most coveted in the English language) is a badge of introversion, the gold standard for most writers. Could anything feel more blessedly gratifying than to send your spit-shined ideas out ahead of you—not depending one whit on how you look or what effortful conversation you cobble together or even how your speaking voice comes across?

I can't now recall many phone conversations I felt good about afterward. I've usually felt the opposite—a little sick, embarrassed for my gushy habit of trying too hard to sound lovable or witty. And I can't even remember my words. What did I say? Was I an ass? Probably.

Deep in the costume trunk of long-ago identities, I fetch one from early reading—as a teenager, of Lawrence Durrell's *Alexandria Quartet*. Say what you like about Durrell: for a young, innocent literary seeker, his prose and its dreamworld struck like thunder, unveiling a jewel-pile of images and revelations. One character for whom a volume of the *Quartet* was named was Clea, who had in youth been surpassingly beautiful but who later suffered from a disfiguring illness (if I'm remembering right), perhaps a skin disease. She'd chosen to live out her remaining life in total isolation, so as not to be seen. *All Clea did was write letters.* And I remember thinking (as a young woman) furiously hard about this arrangement—about the way of life it enforced. In those days I'd thought, *how terrible; she cannot go embrace her true love in the bright light of day.* Now, as an older woman whose face quickly and reliably announces its age, I think, *whoa, excellent! How freeing and empowering to only write letters!*

Maxwell's eccentric interview habit may have annoyed or baffled some of his interlocutors. But he, too, was aging in those years. I don't mean that he worried his face looked old—rather that he'd arrived to a cut-the-crap period of his life (a perfect working definition of the Late Work zone). Typing out his thoughts was the cleanest, most honest way to get things said. He cared nothing about giving offense. He said what he meant.

Maxwell (no surprise) adored letters all his days, and wrote volumes of them. Several collections were published (Sylvia Townsend Warner and Eudora Welty among his many celebrated correspondents). One of the glorious elements of all those exchanges were Maxwell's naked declarations of love for his recipients, both men and women, expressed with a kind of heart-twisting gentleness—worrying for their illnesses and weathers and partners and families; exulting for their triumphs and joys. One senses that his emotional vulnerability humbled many of his friends—especially the men. The beloved

Irish writer Frank O'Connor, who, marvelously for us, was also a cherished correspondent of Maxwell's, holds his own in the two men's warm, affecting collection *The Happiness of Getting It Down Right*.

O'Connor also wrote a revered book about short stories and short story writers, called *The Lonely Voice: A Study of the Short Story*. That book's main title alone has always summarized for me almost everything worth knowing about the entire writing world, and its populace.

I'd argue that the letters we prize over time derive from an emblematic image combining those two men's preoccupations: the lonely voice in its bathrobe. The bathrobe signifies Maxwell's pajama dictum but also—most importantly—the aura of dropping one's guard, shedding protective layers, ease and breathability. One thinks of an actor collapsing in the dressing room after a performance. The guise has been dumped, along with constrictions. The writer's marrow nature— free to flow, seethe, ferment—is spoken by the lonely voice.

The lonely voice cries out to be heard, met, and—in some great, gettin'-up morning—known.

Art makes, and sometimes answers, that effort. O'Connor was, as noted, talking about the essence of short stories and their authors when he coined his title. But letters are driven by the same impulse. Both address a single, trusted witness, real or imagined.

It's consistently clear that the act of *saying* still holds power— despite the floods of garbage avalanching us. I can never forget the parable of Midas going to a barber who couldn't help noticing the king's asses' ears (punishment by Apollo for judging a music contest the wrong way). Sworn to secrecy by Midas but unable to contain it, the barber went out and whispered the fact to a fallow field. When grass grew there, it whispered *Midas has asses' ears* into the wind for all to know.

Which brings me to secrets, and letters that carry them.

Whatever You May Do

I had a brilliant uncle—the late, distinguished professor Joseph Frank (not the Dostoevsky scholar), my father's brother—who'd secured a doctoral degree and was teaching college French by the age of nine-teen. My dear dad, no slouch himself as a Columbia grad who also became a college teacher, claimed that Joe had forgotten more than he, my dad, would ever know. Joe spoke several languages fluently, had read everything, had traveled everywhere, and had served for a period in some diplomatic capacity to Eleanor Roosevelt. (A big glossy photo buried in my family's stashed boxes shows the two beaming together as he steadies before her a document she is sign-ing.) I dimly recall, through conversations with now-dead family members, that Joe had later worked for Voice of America. Then, somehow, he'd been ejected from that heroic organization. A sympa-thetic friend later found him a position teaching at an elite, progres-sive prep school in Colorado. I visited Joe there when I was in high school—too young and self-immersed to have the wits or courage to ask him (or my father) about his past. Joe died in the middle of heart surgery shortly after my visit. He had summoned my father to be with him, sensing he would not make it. My father, bereft, wrote an impas-sioned encomium listing his beloved older brother's astounding achievements. "Wild with grief," my poor dad was. I, his clueless, self-immersed daughter, felt sad for him—confused, intimidated— and vaguely ashamed of the complexity and power of what I sensed I could not yet understand. I still can't imagine how I'd have framed what I wanted to ask Joe. But I've never forgotten my dear dad one day repeating something Joe had told him privately—presumably in anguish and despair:

Whatever you may do—never write down that which you do not wish the whole world to know.

I'd already understood, wordlessly, that my handsome, wise, gen-tle, kind, lonely uncle, who perished at only fifty-three (though, alas, appearing far older) was gay. But in those days one never dared speak of that. Jobs, families, paychecks, reputations depended on silence and discretion. Yet it didn't require much imagination to connect the dots. I believe Joe was fired from Voice of America, or perhaps from a similar distinguished position, when someone intercepted a love let-ter from him to another man.

Having told that sad story: I still believe the letter form will always serve as a conduit for secrets. That's its magnetism: the kernel of its lure. Each configuration—who's writing whom, when, where—stands for itself while comprising a larger pattern. Each carries its sets of conditions and risks, the variousness of personalities making choices inside those contexts. Each contains options for selective censorship, spin, camouflage, embellishment. But each also contains, as shown by my late uncle's case, potential seeds of self-destruction. A writer selects tools for offering her secrets in letters just as she might in making fiction or essays: tone, diction, focus, selective payout. She will tend, I think, to be aware of the stakes. And for whatever reasons we can imagine or guess, she may choose to risk them. That risk may have to do with the mighty power, the incomparable relief, of getting things said. After decades of news cycles bristling with career-toppling scandals from leaked email, texts, and tweets—you would suppose people might resolve to be more careful.

You would be wrong. The lonely voice in its bathrobe cries out—occasionally in foolish, all-too-human error. Listen.

You've Made It

My dear friend gaped at me across the dinner table, her earnest gray eyes wide with admiration and love.

"You've made it," she breathed.

The woman's like a sister to me. I've known her many, many years. I love and admire her. She's a brilliant research scientist—wise, empathic—and has raised three superb kids. She is loyal and faithful, funny and wise.

Bless her: she's less conversant with, say, ambient realities of literary publishing.

We were talking at dinner about the fact that I was bringing out three books that year, via three small publishers.

Here's a bit more background and foreground: I've been writing for thirty years. My body of work (including those latest three) now totals twelve books.

Also, I have no money. I live on Social Security. My retired husband's pension pays our bills. "Royalties" was never a familiar term. All book-related travel, lodging, copies of books for consignment or groups—snacks and drinks at readings—must be purchased by me.

It's the "literary" designation that enforces this.

That particular, mad year—2020—stood out: the year of COVID-19 to be sure, but also a year during which three new books of mine were entering the world. I remain proud of them. It took untellable amounts of time to find publishing homes for them. I'd offered two of them to the same contests repeatedly until one day, to my amazement, they won.

For the last of those three, it took fifteen years of bush-beating to locate an enthusiastic publisher.

That's not a typo. Fifteen.

So when another dear friend, an English teacher, also empathic and bright, suggested that I had "finally got what I wanted," I looked at her with the same blank incredulity my face assumed when my scientist friend breathed, "You've made it."

"No," I said to each woman slowly, carefully, my face confounded with sadness and something close to pitying compassion.

No, I did not get what I wanted.

Both looked at me, uncomprehending. To them, a new book with my name on it should by rights be the ball game. *Three* new books must mean *jackpot*.

What then, asked Friend Number Two, did "getting what I wanted" look like?

My answer popped forth as if memorized—which it has been for some time now:

"A contract with a major house. A modest advance."

Sadly, that answer, in our literary moment, engages a whopping level of fantasy.

Once, long ago, in a state of innocence (encouraged by eager articles in writers' magazines), I was convinced I would eventually find an agent who loved and believed in my work—enough to sell it to a large, respected literary publisher. With publication—naturally—would come good critical recognition. With that would come another contract or sale. In this way (I reasoned) my artistic trajectory would unfurl, and I'd make at least a small bit of money into the bargain.

Alas. Such dreams are now remnants—like historic fabric swatches—of a bygone era: like that (in my mind at least) of Katherine Anne Porter, whom I imagine placing a story in her mailbox, going indoors to paint her nails, and returning to the mailbox a few days later to extract a check.

Those dreams may still occur—but for literary writers, it's almost insanely rare. Grasping this reality happened for me in the previously described, Hemingway mode: slowly, then extra fast.

Thus, I have no agent. I gave up that search after many years. Hundreds of agents praised but declined my offered work ("too literary"). I entered contests instead, and eventually won five of them. All my publishers are small, literary, or university presses. They've been conscientious, legitimate—meaning not author-funded—and yes, very small. I quietly explain, to anyone who asks, that this situation fairly summarizes my lot and my oeuvre—and those of countless others.

Contests gave me small publishers, which gave me a body of work.

Please know I'm truly thankful my books exist. I'm thankful for those brave, small publishers, and for the literary contest victories that allowed me to build an oeuvre.

But "making it" is not how I'd describe what has happened.

When I see authors today receiving big splashes of publicity in major media, or agents selling new works to major houses for six-figure sums, or (harshest cut) someone's Facebook photo of their pending contract with a respected house—I try to muster mental and emotional distance to cheer for them. Even so—the unasked *How?* murmurs uneasily inside most writers' minds when they view such splashes. Sometimes it's luck. Sometimes someone knew someone. Each splash represents a huge bet by the publisher, as with racehorses. Sometimes the bet triumphs. Often, not so much.

Now: if you've already dwelt inside this game for some while, you'll wearily recognize all the above. And you'll know there's only one cul-de-sac where these thoughts must end up.

It's the constant re-reckoning, the existential dusting of hands, the hitching-up of pants. (Emphasis on "constant.")

First, consider the modest advance. Why seek money? Everyone knows that not only does literary writing bring little or no money: it actually *costs* a writer (see above-cited duties to buy copies of her own books, spring for travel and board, snacks and drinks at readings, on and on; many authors deplete their personal savings to pay thousands for a publicist). Partly, one asks for money because one wants to be accorded a basic dignity: *This is my warranted profession and its real product, my booth in the marketplace.* In the same spirit, one seeks even token compensation for specialized services: *your doctor, dentist, and plumber will not work for free.* But more deeply, writers seek money for another reason. Richard Bausch is eloquent in one of his passionate Reprises (occasional paragraphs of writerly advice on social media). Italics are mine:

> One of the most endearing things about all the writers I know . . . is that . . . [t]hey want money of course . . . but when they get it they use it mostly to buy one thing: *Time. That's all any of them want.* To be able to purchase a little Time from the world's daily demands, and they want that time, all of them that I know, *for one reason. To work. No material matter comes close to that for them.* . . . [W]e all share . . . that sweet almost child-like quality of wanting from the world only a little time to keep doing this thing we love so much that even when it tortures us we long to be there in it and with it.

What's more: fame and notoriety, even the most star-spangled, can prove fleeting. In his *Poets & Writers* article "Author Envy: The Art of Surviving One's Own Personality," William Giraldi notes (italics mine): "Some of those writers with all the laurels and grants and sales today will likely not be remembered in thirty years, never mind in three hundred, so you have to put it to yourself: *What's your intention with literature? What do you want from it?* Are you an artist because you cannot be otherwise, because it is essential to your soul and mind and your vista on our world, or because you want cheers from strangers and plaudits from the lit establishment?"

To deflect a knee-jerk wisecrack: Yes. Most of us, despite the screamingly consistent realities, want both, thanks: the soul-feeding, world-view part, *and* the cheers and plaudits part. Few cop to that. And sure as eggs, we get disabused of this secret longing around the clock. (Read Don Lee's fearless account called "What's the Point of Writing if You're Not Going to Succeed?" in *Electric Literature*.)

Giraldi suggests we'd do better to aim our disgruntlement at those who seek to thwart writers and art in general. That's noble. But to me it's also a red herring. To me the monolithic *Why do you do this* forces focus: draws the predicament's true, eternal bottom line.

"It is not your fault, it is not my fault, that I write," observes the immortal James Baldwin in *The Cross of Redemption: Uncollected Writings*. "And I never would come before you in the position of a complainant for doing something that I must do."

Something that I must do. No more nor less.

No one holds a gun to our heads. No writing police (this image, famously, from Anne Lamott) bash down the door at 4 a.m. demanding new work. The whole gambit's still an act of free will, against tragicomic odds. And our energies and well-being, as we keep doing it, are never promised protection at any level.

Why is it, I keep wondering—and now I'm going to italicize because it bothers me enough to shout—why must we have to *reidentify and reabsorb the above hard truths again and again?* Because hysterical culture drowns them out. It's hard to think clearly while the volume's turned up. I confess it feels more difficult than ever, lately, simply to turn back to the work—let all the noise, dust, and confetti flutter past.

Yet that's always the task: to understand (over and over) it's our choice.

Nothing else is given. Rump parked in chair, hands poised over paper or keyboard: the only sanctuary, the only solace, the only control; the place where one feels purposeful, defined, alive. Don Lee cites the excruciating example of his late mentor, Richard Yates, who battled terrible conditions in his lifetime and suffered hellishly: "It was what he did. It was who he was. He kept writing, even when there were so few rewards to do so, even when the work was hard, and lonely, and unfulfilling. It was his life. It was his calling."

Conjoined to the above grim report? A lifetime's gorgeous reading. Piles and piles of heavenly books—each of which I take up at day's end like a hymnal and, once sung through, murmuring or thinking, *thank you.*

So: technically? Making good work, and reading others' beautiful works, are certainly what I have wanted—never stopped wanting. *And I have made sure, somehow, that I always did get them.*

But in addition?

I contain multitudes. I will always feel badly—a species of real grief—about *not making it*. And I will bet a huge portion of anything you've got (beer, marbles, candy) that no matter how well they behave or how successful we may assume them to be, bazillions of good writers in their secret hearts feel exactly the same.

The simultaneous, not-so-secret secret is, there's no bloody choice.

Except that's not strictly true. There's always a choice.

Thus, we to have to re-choose and re-choose: repeatedly, constantly. To borrow the infamous line from Flannery O'Connor's *A Good Man is Hard to Find*, we need to be shot to death every minute of our lives.

Make It Go Away

Q uick: What's the first goal for a writer—for artists, for anyone—
living in a time of worldwide plague?

Easy, on the face of it: Survive. Keep strong. Stay well, and alert.

Shut up and do everything it takes. Care for beloveds. Minimize risk. Obey the Surgeon General. Stay put. Get the vaccine when it shows up. Get the booster. Get the kids vaxxed.

Repeat.

The consistent fantasy—oh, how we all long for it—is to look back on the scourge in relief. Trading memories of how it was.

At this writing, we're barely able to keep up with the now.

That's become—putting it gently—the trickier task.

For this moment, breaking revelations still blizzard down nonstop, burying us past our eyebrows. By revelations I don't just mean the progress of vaccines, political wars, riots and insurrections, gossip, ecological cataclysm, mortality numbers, or dwindling hospital beds.

I mean revelations about meaning. Hide-and-seek with meaning.

With the advents of all the above, meaning itself seems to mutate almost hourly, twisting, wrinkling, shredding. Life's under siege. Nothing can feel the same from the moment one steps outside the door—though if you squint, things on their surfaces appear familiar. It's what's directly beneath those surfaces that decimates. The news screams *death, destruction, chaos.* Our minds struggle to look straight at it.

Unsurprisingly, our responses have popped forth in waves, a surging of flung-open jack-in-the-boxes. We've had terrible trouble sleeping. We've experienced bad dreams, anxiety, stress; muzziness; depression, manic panic. We've felt spaced out or angry or glum, tired or twitchy, scared or numb or listless; wanting to eat or drink ourselves insensible or just stop eating and never get out of bed. We've burst into tears at fluky moments. Former goals (productivity, social gestures, acquiring things) have flattened and bled out, unrecognizable as road kill.

The known world shrank to the size of domestic floor space. Fastidiousness segued into neurosis, childlike irritability, and straight-up freakouts. You're standing right where I want to be. I like *that* cup best. Get dressed? Why?

Analogies for lockdown realities have varied. One is Anne Frank's attic. Another is living under house arrest. Another—repeated ad nauseam like the particulars of our days themselves—is the movie *Groundhog Day*, which I'd only reprise here to highlight one refinement. Our predicament is best captured, I think, by one crucial cut in that film—to the scene in which Bill Murray calmly reads a book at the lunch counter of the local diner. With that inspired shot (which no one, to my knowledge, has yet singled out for major praise) we're slammed by the totality of Murray's character's surrender. Forced to accept his entrapment, sentenced to live out the same day into eternity, he's done a poignantly existential thing.

He's made himself at home inside it.

To a large degree, many of us have done the same. We've resigned ourselves to reading quietly at the eternal lunch counter.

It's consoling—sort of—to find oneself inducted into a huge club by default. But that does not change the unspeakable conditions of membership. A dear friend commented wisely: "I know we're lucky and that so many people we know are lucky [to have] good health, homes, enough food, etc. It sometimes strikes me that complaining is a luxury. Even so, I complain—and malls are closing and small businesses can't pay rent, so the outside world is a twisted art installation of shuttered doors."

It may be that when this thing is past—if it will ever be past—we'll promise each other never to forget it, to be and act and do better.

Then we'll quickly forget every last speck of that and go back to being heedless, grabbing idiots. It is possible.

Meantime? The prime internal bulletin for me, during the deep-vault exile of lockdown, has been one I don't see a slew of writers admitting.

A saggy joke throughout this pandemic, from well-meaning friends and family referring to us writers—well known to be introverts, cranks, hermits—went like this:

"Jeez, you must be in heaven. You don't have to go anywhere or see anyone. You can live in your pajamas and eat popcorn and write your heart out."

Cue everyone's sour laughter. Utterers of the quip sounded proud of its fresh wit, waiting for the writer to find it hilarious, too.

Technically, it's true. We've gone straight to the work every day. We've maybe felt some guilty thankfulness for being able to do it without preamble or apology.

But that's where the joke breaks down. Have writers viewed this new, enforced working time as perfect heaven? Did we feel clear and righteous about whatever we'd been tapping out in our plague-buffered hidey-hole?

Yeah—no, I don't think so. No. Would you easily celebrate hunkering down at the notebook or keyboard while an asteroid sped toward earth, or a tidal wave raced toward your home? Feel compelled to restyle interior decor in the *Titanic*'s cabins?

I couldn't. Can't.

No question, in the old days certain jolly distractions—travel and recreations imposed by my dear spouse and innocent others—seemed a zombie conspiracy to drink my blood, to block my love affair with reading and writing.

Yet if you asked any number of writers during a plague year, I'm suspecting they might well confess the unspeakable, as I do here:

We've missed everything and everyone. Teeth-chatteringly.

That could, I know, be another way of saying we've missed the enemy.

We've missed Zorba's "full catastrophe": the pulse and chaos of life, the fussing and yammering, juggling and chafing. The endless, draining noise and dance.

I can't believe I'm saying this, but I've missed ground-level hubbub—even if it was always *something I routinely fought*. Like Kingsley Amis's battleships laboring to turn around at sea, I've begun to grasp the stunning lesson of plague time: the utter primacy to us as animals, of *gathering*.

Take away gathering; little remains. Commerce, services, systems implode or go wonky—and with them, culture, and close behind that, mental health. Without familiar shapes, motions, and networks, we lose our bearings. Who'd guess that even within the saddest, most people-hating hearts lurked an actual, physical longing to hug and be hugged (even those lucky enough to live with a beloved partner)? Some of us have also painfully missed the very small beings (not, alas, in our pods) whom we once could unthinkingly hold in our arms. By the time we can safely hold them again, we fear they may be grown.

We've missed thoughtless, intermingled, physical, busy, abrasive, stupid, forceful, exalted life.

I never could have accepted this, had I not felt it.

But the revelation goes deeper. It's been about more than animal hunger to hang out and be held.

What's also gone mushy and mealy is identity. One defines oneself, as a rule, against a witnessing backdrop. If you say to a wino crumpled on the curb *hey, I'm a writer*, they might or might not deign to grunt back at you. But you'll have named a calling in recognizable language before a fellow member of your species. Something happens. You've defined yourself—if only for yourself—before another's gaze, another's sensibility, however briefly or messily.

If witnesses vanish, do we exist? Crisp boundaries loosened during lockdown, disassembled, floated off in motes. This weightlessness seems related to the riddle of a tree falling in a forest with no one near to hear. It also feels connected to the futility of dressing in street clothes—*street* suddenly such a telling designation—or wearing makeup or jewelry. By extension: Why fuss with meals? Why arrange the green beans in their own little pile beside the veggie burger? Why anything? Why not just stare out the window watching the light change for, oh, twelve or fourteen months?

(Bathing, I do hope, won't fall by the wayside.)

Parents raising kids? You're hereby given a complete pass on everything. Not for you such lazy dithering. More: you deserve medals and prizes. The same for health-care workers; also service workers, first responders, and everyone on the front lines: everyone who'll have acted, in Mr. Rogers's words, as a Helper.

At the beginning of all this, an astronaut wrote an article advising us that if she could live in space alone for a year, we could manage living in isolation under lockdown. She itemized her principles: make a routine, exercise, care for your brain and emotional health; stay connected. Turns out these sane basics did not prove so easily adaptable by earthbound types. Are we inferior creatures? Certainly, later historians will feast on the naughty-nice list of our small triumphs and cavernous failures. And without doubt a ton of zingy post-facto studies will appear, like thousand-piece human-nature puzzles (shadows of *Lord of the Flies* flickering through the window).

Except, reader? To hell with it.

Like everyone, I never wanted to be part of this experiment. I want back the simple luxury of fighting people for private time. I crave the clarity of knowing, without an avalanche of second (third, hundredth) thoughts, what I'm doing and why. I want to embrace friends while eating and drinking with them—if later grumbling about them.

More than anything I want people to stop getting sick and dying, to get jobs, food, health care, schools, and decent life restored to them.

In the words of my then-very-young stepson when my husband, telling him stories, channeled a scary invented ogre named Mr. Meany:

"Make it go away!"

It's worth noting here that in many an artist's heart a tremendous deadlock has raged, around which all the above-named commotion twirls—like that symbol for medical doctors with its famed upright sword entwined (menaced) by snakes.

How can writing—any art—matter during mortal terror?

Who wants to make up stories or discuss vagaries of style when people are dying in swaths? What can any of us produce that will be of real use—or even make sense in this context?

Cue the slow, deep breath. Cue the lowered head.

Multiple times the above question has reared its own, big, angry head. And my reflex each time is to cave, conceding the worst: that mere art, during a plague, can make no more difference than morning dew—that it can scarcely matter. If bombs are falling, how puny art *must* seem.

Yet in the next instant I'm forced to remember the heroism of European museum curators who, during war years, evacuated precious inventories and hid or buried them in secret locales until it was safe to exhume them. How this fact repeatedly fills us with wonder as we gaze on incalculable treasures, generations later.

Then I begin to think about our own personal choices, daily, hourly, for the use of time during isolation—with no observer taking notes or cocking a gun at us.

I notice *what I've seen myself reach for* constantly as comfort, nourishment, reinforcement. And from their reports, a lot of friends have appeared to be doing pretty much the same.

I've reached for music, films, and books. Simple as that.

I've never stopped playing the music I love, Bach to Barbosa-Lima. Evenings we've watched movies that distracted, beautified, stirred, soothed, or made us laugh like maniacs. Documentaries. Dance. If anything made me happy-cry, so much the better.

But above all I've been constantly immersed in the reading I sensed would fortify me, the language that would feel immutable— even if bombs fell.

This reading has included some horrific material, stories others might consider nihilistic or creepy. Carson McCullers's *Reflections in a Golden Eye* (my paperback edition introduced with fierce relish by Tennessee Williams) proved as powerful a nightmare as they come. Yet something about its calm recital of human peculiarity and darkness felt like release, invigorating as lungfuls of Swiss air. The terrible truths embedded in every word of its eerie murder story—of jealousy, erotic confusion, inchoate mortal longing—reassured. I couldn't question this odd chemistry. Most of what I've been reading could not have been written to address someone stranded in frightened isolation during a plague year. Yet there was no escaping the awareness that the material had been written because it had to be written. Thus, the writing that most mattered felt as if it had been murmured in the dark to a secret friend—me—with that gorgeous one-on-one intensity that reverberates in a reader's skull.

Meredith Hall's novel *Beneficence*, an epic, bittersweet saga chronicling an American farm family's ordeals during the early twentieth century, was one such discovery. So was Nicole Krauss's dreamlike yet ruthlessly cerebral story collection *To Be a Man*, and Robert Hass's book of glittering, gritty poetry, *Summer Snow*. Wright Morris's *Plains Song* (I'm late to it) struck me as wondrous. I was swept away by Peter Cameron's dark, austere, nearly perfect *What Happens at Night*, and wished it would never end.

Other reading that "gave good weight" during plague time included Henri Troyat's brilliant, bristling biography, *Tolstoy*. (Troyat got around. Check his eye-poppingly vast oeuvre.) Another was Rachel Cohen's deep dive into her own experience, interleaved with that of Jane Austen, in *Austen Years*. Another still was Margot Livesey's luminously compassionate *The Boy in the Field*.

I've got a queue of waiting titles at the library (curbside pickup) as tall as I am. In that queue are some surprises, if what I've cited sounds too draconian. I've ordered plenty of fiction (Ayad Akhtar, Charles Yu, Yang Huang, Robert Jones Jr.) but also essays: *Homo Irrealis*, Andre Aciman; *My Lives*, Edmund White; *The Way of Bach*, Dan Moller. *Wintering*, Katherine May. Daniel Mendelsohn's *An Odyssey* blew me away.

Underpinning works like the above runs a series of impulses to reabsorb some timeless icons. The Russians. Shirley Hazzard. Marguerite Yourcenar. Tove Jansson. Virginia Woolf (*A Writer's Diary* was written while real bombs fell, and describes them).

Not every title succeeds. I've had to abandon some. It's a waste of time to pretend otherwise. Focus is still skittery, mindful of plague news. And time's still precious, even as it sucks and swells and bubbles like lava. The oldest criterion applies: Given horrific straits, what insists we stick around? What reaches into us; what puts something back? Engagement's slipperier than ever, in light of pulverized attention spans. I'm after whatever holds me—aware, too, that for plenty of others this might mean video games.

As my canny young granddaughter notes, shrugging: "What're you gonna do?"

Maybe good art (in any form) fixes a hard ground floor of honesty that can be stood upon calmly while the planet shudders; a sturdy roof when the heavens open: *Here is the church, here is the steeple.* The titles that feel talismanic, as if they emit lifesaving signals, demand we hold them close: *Here's who we are. Here's who we've been. Here's what we have meant and can still, may still, mean.* Certain books act like emergency-relief parcels dropped straight into the yearning heart. Their voices—all some version, per Louise Glück, of "the solitary human voice, raised in lament or longing"—still talk to me, telling me things it helps to remember while the shitstorm rages outside. In truth, the exact same chemistry applies, post-shitstorm. It's the only answer to inarticulable anguish I can locate for now—one I'll keep taking as I find it.

Naked Emperors

W e can't do this, but I will.
　　 We can't talk about what I'm going to talk about without becoming sidelined by the problem of taste—something already nearly hopeless in literary realms.

Too bad. I'm going ahead with it.

Full disclosure: My own literary taste remains as old-fashioned as they come—language-driven, style-framed, skewed toward a certain moral ethos or ambience. Call that ambience a kind of questing interiority. I'm a bloodhound snuffling for the secret heart of each work—the *It of Its*, a friend and I once termed it—the thing that's new news even if it treats the oldest concerns on earth, which will speak to me in my bones.

Nonetheless I swear it's possible—desirable—to temporarily wall off the issue of taste to focus on a recent (at this writing), terribly troubling literary event.

An essay called "These Precious Days" by Ann Patchett appeared in the longstanding, high-end, highbrow *Harper's Magazine*, causing a tremendous, impassioned fanfare. I was urged to read the piece by one of my dearest, oldest friends—my high school English teacher; an exceptionally kind, patient, discerning man. He thought he was handing me a gift. I'd already noticed that a number of writers in my social media network, many of whom are fairly high-profile and whom I hugely admire, adored this essay.

I mean: They were melting for it. Worshipping it.

Patchett is famous—someone whose work is not my favorite but whom I've always respected; assumed to be smart, awake, aware.

The essay horrified me.

Why? Because it broke, or fouled, a basic covenant of serious literary writing.

The molested covenant is this: A writer's words represent her bond. The printed words—especially in a distinguished venue—translate as a warrant:

This is my best, deepest truth, told as well as I can. I stand by it.

If we disagree with a piece of writing—clash with its ideas or its style—that's fine, even expected. Writing's life, especially that of essays, ought to provoke and disturb. Worthy work may or may not persuade, but it inspires critical thought.

If the piece as a whole intention, however, strikes us as elaborately dishonest—*at the expense of its human subject*—that's something else.

You'll correctly guess it's the second category I'm naming—and by which I'm sickened. The disappointment hits hard because—first, as noted, Patchett's renowned, and skilled. But second and far more strangely: I assumed that people who know better—an arts-craving demographic, many of them artists themselves—would surely have instantly seen the problem.

They should have called the emperor naked.

The piece starts cheerfully. Patchett meets and gets friendly with the ultra-beloved movie star, Tom Hanks.

(This opening soured me straightaway because it seemed to brag: "Here is the level of star I am known to hang out with." I read on.)

Patchett soon befriends Hanks's kind, thoughtful, self-effacing personal assistant, whose first name is Sooki.

Cutting short an insanely long story: Sooki becomes Patchett's email pen pal.

At some point, we learn that Sooki has been diagnosed with cancer.

Patchett goes to enormous, personal, complicated lengths to help Sooki.

That's the gist of it.

Many, many, *many* activities, thoughts, and comments follow.

The two become closer in the course of this excruciating arc, though—heaven knows with good reason—Sooki quietly, firmly guards a certain threshold of privacy.

By the piece's end, no one knows how her various treatments (including clinical trials at state-of-the-art medical centers) will play out.

But Patchett has, during this account, built a palace of self-regard and led us through dozens of its shimmering rooms.

She does this by describing her frantic efforts to help: acceleratingly dramatic, labyrinthine efforts. Each detail pulses with intensifying urgency. Patchett ultimately houses Sooki, feeds her, procures travel for her, collects lost objects, tracks every medical report and prognostication, makes bazillion careful arrangements, and devises and performs countless frantic—not to say desperate—actions on Sooki's behalf.

They do yoga together.

Because the story was concurrent with COVID-19's rampant hold on the country and world, the virus and its restrictions also frame this narrative, tightening tensions and pumping stakes. Things rollercoaster along. I won't itemize each new crisis here (dozens) because that would amount to paraphrasing the entire piece, which went on so long that by the time I finally arrived to its last lines I felt almost ill—not from sympathetic symptoms but from exhaustion. Patchett builds a plot in which fear, and efforts to stanch fear, double and redouble. A powerful anguish looms up and sways before us like a kind of Godzilla, crashing around, shrieking.

What I could not shake, pushing through paragraph after paragraph of this colossal, dense, grains-of-sand-parsed, moment-by-moment, hair-on-fire report—which also recruits the goodhearted clout of Patchett's doctor husband—is the stunned numbness that gathers in a reader under the unceasing lash of its demand: Pay attention. Pay attention. Pay *lavish attention.* Longer, expository lines interleave with short, powerful sentences: the breaking-news *pow-pow-pow* of it shocks readers into a daze, helpless not to track every note, praying its audible sweep will soon, somehow, land.

It doesn't land. The sweep simply halts.

Then it evaporates.

At its close, the kind, wearied Sooki seems at least to be holding steady following treatments. In an email she pays modestly grateful tribute to Patchett, noting the author's "specialness."

Finally Patchett murmurs, essentially, "No one knows what will happen."

These last words, dropped like a coy hankie, are presented almost as a sly triumph. Patchett is perfectly aware of having built dramatic momentum to a near-unbearable frenzy. She's aware that the reader is by then panting, drained, crazed with worry, awaiting any least reassurance, let alone closure. And Patchett seems almost—almost—to be *mocking* a reader's need for that by halting the piece as and when she does, puttying up its gaping-open end with a hasty line or two about the windfall bonus of late-life friendship.

In fairness, this essay bore a subtitle suggesting there'd be no definitive ending, to wit: "Tell Me How the Story Ends."

The piece might have been more accurately subtitled *I made a friend. Things got hard, and then harder. Reader, that's all I got.*

The friendship, and Patchett's exertions, may be real. That's not enough.

There's been a violation. The piece, at some awful level, feels slightly immoral.

It is dishonest because it never cops to its own, appalling subtext: Patchett's heroism. Behind its breathless striving and anxious scheming, all those infinitesimally documented, acrobatic, and emotional swoops to fix and fortify, Patchett is saying, *This is me; this is how I roll. I do good. Look at me doing good.*

Cancer or no, friendship or no: this screed cannot stand as fair for what it gobbles of a reader's faith, time, and care—and for its shameless self-display: the floor show of Patchett itemizing her own rescue operations. My reaction has nothing to do with caring for the fate of Sooki, who sounds like a superb human being and whom I pray will survive and thrive. But in this essay, poor Sooki's survival has somehow been *commandeered as a measuring instrument for Patchett's self-display.*

My reaction is gut-born from a lifetime of love and respect for language—including an instinct of rearing back from the pungent smell of its fraudulent use.

In the words of *Madeline*'s Miss Clavel: Something is not right.

Self-aggrandizement under a veil of blow-by-blow derring-do can't be moral.

Clearly, Patchett has no clue about the size or substance of her error. I cannot understand why. This author's been on the literary scene for years. She is surely as porous as any writer alive to human nuance, turns of language, layers of motives and behavior. Yet she appears serenely unconscious for thirty-some pages of her material's effect: behind an intricate fan-dance of helping it is wildly self-glorifying; a lengthy, bloated boast at the expense of an innocent, struggling friend.

I spoke of my horrified bewilderment with a friend who is herself an accomplished author—and who reacted to this essay as I did.

"What," she wondered in an email, "were the magazine's editors smoking?"

I think the editors were smoking a brand of marketing called (by a prominent magazine editor in a blunt moment) The Names. Meaning, famous writers. To paraphrase a movie line: *If you run The Names, readers will come.* The magazine's editors must have figured: *Patchett's well known, well loved, and into the bargain she is pals with an adored, megawatt movie star.*

Again: for me the fundamental wonder of this piece was why more smart readers—so many of them also sensitive writers—did not instantly see through it and call it out.

My friend answered gently: "Even the smartest among us—maybe also the kindest—are susceptible . . . and lose full command of [our] otherwise sharp critical faculties because the famous person's glow is so blinding." It seems people feel bound to preserve and protect what they believe they most admire. Therefore, anything coming from a beloved author must be meaningful and, yes, lovable.

Another friend—this one a veteran of her own hair-raising medical challenges—was instinctively repelled by the essay. She volunteered this reaction:

It occurs to me that if good manners are (somehow) to endure, we are responsible for calling out bad behavior and upholding truth whenever and wherever we can. . . . Personally, I don't think Patchett and Sooki ever [truly] became friends. Patchett [sounds] more like the B&B host who interferes so much you're happy to hear the thunk of the door on a Marriott the next time you travel.

What comforts me most is this friend's bemusement:

It's beyond my understanding that the literary community is ga-ga over this—yes—violation.

I've cross-examined myself. Have I pulled similar stunts in my own work? Have I insisted behind and between lines, *Look at me, look what I did, look how good I am*? Do most writers occasionally stumble into this pothole? Might it explain why the much-praised, endless, messy diatribe in *Harper's* smashed such a major nerve in me?

Yeah—no: I've done plenty of stupid things in my work, but I can't make that particular case. The reason's too real, too close: I could never, respecting a reader's trust, deliberately construct a show *guest-starring my own glorious generosity.*

Readers pour so much care, so much distilled attention into writing by authors they admire. They are "bustling about," in Sven Birkerts's lovely words, building the story in their minds detail for detail as they read. They deserve, as they come away from a long, dense work—from any work—to be left with more than simply to contemplate *what a wondrously selfless hero its author has proved herself to be.* Because of course if that's the rub, the opposite's been true: self has been the author's meat and drink the entire while.

No human suffering serious illness deserves to be exploited this way—as an ersatz documentary subject who's instead deputized as a decoy for the real subject—its author.

As for the torrent of admiration it triggered? Sometimes, it appears, we decide to see what we need to see.

Yet both reader and author deserve to emerge together with something received from an honest reckoning. They deserve to feel that the taking in and assimilating of the world they just traversed comprised a better, deeper truth than the one they left behind.

Ready or Not

The following account could, for some of us, perhaps compete with Ford Madox Ford's notion of a "saddest story ever told."

It may also strike fellow writers as too familiar.

Everyone else? Talk among yourselves.

This is the story of making a book—more precisely, of what followed after the book was written. It happened a long time ago, here on Earth.

I finished the novel in a kind of molten state, determined to get it told following the death of a beloved, complex friend. Its arc may echo that of William Stoner in the brilliant John Williams novel by that name, as it narrates a quiet, self-effacing life that might otherwise have slipped invisibly past—been ignored, mocked, or scorned.

Stoner's trajectory can read as bewildering for the relentless pile-up of ordeals inflicted upon its namesake. They are ordeals that find—against our conventional yearning—no resolution, no justification, no rationales. *Stoner* is not an easy nor a comforting read. But it stands like a titan amid its literary brethren: a quiet jewel, a thing apart whose numinousness only intensifies as we revisit it over years.

Needless to say: If you've not yet absorbed *Stoner* and you love literary fiction, please do yourself the extreme favor of finding it. Then please read Steve Almond's impassioned consideration, *William Stoner and the Battle for the Inner Life*.

As it happens, though, I had no thought for the two novels' parallelism when I commenced offering my own *Stoner*—ultimately called *The Outlook for Earthlings*.

Like most, I started by submitting the manuscript to literary agents. A long game began—maybe rather a dance—known far too well to most writers: Fiercely Hopeful Petitioner Steps Forward, Meets Radio Silence; Steps Back Pelted by Rejection Coated with Sad Praise.

Hundreds and hundreds of them. Rejections, that is.

At a certain point early on in the agent search, one single soul— still remembered with love by many—said Yes to the novel, in a letter so filled with appreciation I've kept it framed under glass. Her name was Christina "Kit" Ward. I felt convinced, when Kit wrote me, that everything beautiful was about to begin—not least a golden friend-ship. My overflowing heart envisioned a sale and a contract, good critical response followed by another contract, and the same process then repeating ever after.

I felt so certain of success I mailed Kit a magic wand, purchased from a costume store.

Kit could not sell the novel.

She tried to console me by suggesting, very gently, that I adapt a mental stance of subtle detachment from publishers' responses. It had to do, this mental state, she said, with "*not* being *un*attached." I under-stood—fleetingly—what Kit was urging. I still loved her. But I learned that not only could I *not* find such detachment in myself; I couldn't *want* to find it. If desire guaranteed suffering, so be it. I would desire.

A couple of years later, Kit suddenly died.

After a stunned period, I resumed querying agents. What else was there to do? Years of drawn-out trials ensued. Agents took eons to respond—if they responded at all. Often they never did. After fruit-lessly approaching over two hundred of them—and after an extended minuet with one who, capping a year of warm phone calls and editing suggestions, announced that his firm's "fiction committee" had nixed the project—I gave up on agents and began directly seeking any small publisher for the novel.

During this process I became a sort of walking almanac of small, literary presses. I learned their mastheads, profiles, track records. Inevitably, they struggled. Some perished. Others, by turns, kept being born.

I tried to stay abreast. I entered contests.

Rejections continued. Many were framed in language I found cold and cutting. Others contained elaborate expressions of regret, explaining how their tiny operation simply could not take on all the titles it admired. These often also offered lavish praise, much of which I recorded. Some compliments were so good (spoiler here) I wound up using them as blurbs—seventeen years later.

I still have thirty-some pages of those single-spaced, nine-point-type lists of rejections; agents' and publishers' comments and compliments. I'm still not sure why I felt I had to keep such meticulous records—likely in part so as not to repeat myself too soon each time I chose targets for the next volley of submissions. (I queried lots of them more than once over the years.) But I think I also carried within me an instinctive, gathering sense of *building a case* of some kind—of amassing evidence.

At this point, please believe: I'm aware that any reader with a salt-speck of reason will wonder why I persisted. Said reader might also sensibly wonder whether my faith in my own writing (or at least in the novel) didn't begin by then to, say, tremble.

The answer may sound a little monstrous.

I knew the book was difficult. I also knew that any number of "difficult" literary works have never stopped pouring into public view—starting from way, way back—and that many have since wound up being embraced, lauded, even adored.

It might be worth examining *Stoner*'s history for this reason. Reception for the novel wasn't good when Williams brought it out: it scarcely made a ripple before sinking utterly. Critics shrugged; turned up their noses. In a 2014 *New York Times* article about the novel's painful early life, Steve Almond commented:

> Since its publication in 1965, "Stoner" has gone out of print twice, doomed by its mundane plot and restrained style. But a funny thing happened on the way to the remainders table. Thanks to a legion of [latter-day] disciples, many of them prominent writers (along with Tom Hanks, who recommended the book in a Time

interview), "Stoner" became the Little Novel That Could. Despite selling only 2,000 copies in its initial printing, "Stoner" topped best-seller lists all across Europe last year, and has steadily infiltrated literary discussions about the American canon. For the most part . . . this tale of literary resurrection affirms our sense that posterity shouldn't be about publishing trends or marketing budgets. Herman Melville figured "Moby-Dick" would be his masterpiece and was bewildered when it bombed. "The Great Gatsby" was dismissed for years as a minor work. The list goes on. Orwell famously argued that the only real critic of literature is time.

One takes Almond's information to heart and holds it there—let me assure you—damned close. One tells oneself his logic makes sense. Emotionally, however, rejections of *Earthlings* never grew easier to take. Only the praise that also came so reliably with those rejections encouraged me that I had not been insane; had not wrongly believed *Earthlings* a story worth telling.

Still: I could not fathom why people so consistently went to such lengths to glorify the novel while, like clockwork, declining it.

Some editors said, "too literary." What can "literary" mean in this context? We may take turns guessing. Cerebral? Interior? Discomfiting? Guilty on all counts. At the miserable heart of it, I understood what those editors wished to convey: *We can't sell this.* To which I've no good answer except—well, we can also name hundreds, maybe thousands of such works that, by coming into the world, have at least initially justified someone's earnest idea that they should, in fact, exist.

So in a spirit combining stubbornness, routine, and morbid curiosity (how long can this seriously go on?), I kept offering the book. I kept entering contests. I kept recording the dates and language of rejections, and of praise.

At the same time, I never stopped making other work—essays, stories, new novels. For each, of course, I undertook the usual actions to secure publishing homes for them. (The stuff wasn't going to market itself.) Through all of it I also tended, like everyone, to the quotidian human chores, the bills and cleaning, exercise, travel, family, friends, loves and losses: the big pile of Life Spaghetti that enmeshes and entwines us all.

Across those years, submitting *Earthlings* became rote—another daily chore. I also saw it as a method of fishing I had noticed out at Ocean Beach in San Francisco, where I'd lived. Gigantic poles, attached to long lines cast far out to sea, had been propped along the shore in the cold, saline fog, spaced at generous distance from each other. The fisherman in charge of them had stationed a nearby folding chair in the sand alongside a stash of supplies (thermos, food, radio), so he could easily keep his eyes on his lines.

Earthlings, you see, was always one of several fishing lines.

And it just stood there and stood there, while other lines caught things, and were packed up, and new lines were staked.

After still more years, submitting the novel became so seamlessly ingrained, so thoughtless an act of maintenance—like brushing one's teeth or lacing one's sneakers—that I began without consciousness to internalize Kit Ward's original advice: I *almost* lost attachment to any outcome. I had quietly let go of the concept of results—*without ceasing to try*. The reflex had morphed into a soothing ritual—the floor you swept, the pet you fed, before turning to other work.

At some buried level I still guarded the sense that a miracle was possible—that someone might one day take the novel. But that possibility remained so deeply sealed off I dared not exhume it, dared not indulge entertaining it. Doing so might contaminate the fresher hopefulness of energies directed toward making, and offering, new works.

The small publisher that, late one summer fifteen years on, sent an e-letter declaring that it would be delighted to accept *Earthlings*, was very young on the small-press scene—and ambitious.

My sense of the event—after the *whump* of shock chased by disbelief, then distrust; after scanning the publisher's history and checking with a couple of authors it had brought out—was that this publisher's credentials seemed valid.

I wrote my dear friend, a professional in the industry who knows the small-press scene: "Is this a thing?"

Yes, it is, she said. Why not go ahead.

Fifteen years.

Slowly, still dull with disbelief, I began the time-honored exertions of bringing out *Earthlings* as a real, live book.

I contacted authors who agreed to read and blurb it. I pondered cover images. I composed summaries of the story for marketing and jacket-flap copy. I compiled lists of literary venues, local and national media, writing programs, and art residencies to notify.

At some level I remained dazed. These motions, always in service of other works, were actually now happening for *Earthlings*—the eternal stepchild, the ugly duckling.

Is there a punch line?

Glad you asked. There are two.

First, *Earthlings* (and *two* other books of mine, as luck and tragicomic coincidence would arrange it) would be published two years later, in that triply catastrophic year for authors bringing out new work—or for anyone doing anything—2020. A year of pandemic, wildfires, and rabid political, economic, and social agonies.

Life outstrips art, ready or not.

Again, I cannot claim here that I alone have escaped to tell you. Uncountable numbers of writers at every rung of the notoriety ladder had to confront the isolated, Zoom-confined, muffled predicament of publishing a book in 2020. Of course, those other writers may not have waited seventeen years. Then again, who knows?

Please allow this: the reviews of *Earthlings* that emerged, pandemic or no, world cataclysm or no, were heart-mashingly lovely. "Line by line . . . continually stunned us with its grace." "An elegant elegy." "Perhaps [her] best work." "Compulsively readable."

Did fame and fortune appear? That would have made a glorious finish. Alas: fame and fortune seem long ago to have missed the freeway turnoff to my house. Instead, something like a faint mist—say, of wry amusement—effervesces spicily around this tale, like the zest scraped from lemons or ginger-ale bubbles. Maybe that's what "seasoning" means.

I told myself the sequence makes, if nothing more, a story worth telling.

Then came a second shoe, plonking down. At the end of a radio interview by telephone heralding the arrival of *Earthlings*, after I'd confessed the true history of its seventeen years as a bridesmaid, my kind interlocutor remarked:

"Let me ask you this, Joan. Today (he named that day's date), looking back on all your books—what does it make you think? What do you have to say about it?"

Boom.

The question blindsided me. My skull emptied.

Then it filled with (swear to heaven) white light.

A beat later I found myself astonished by the words coming from my own mouth.

"That I've been able to inhabit my calling," I heard my independent mouth say.

Hesitantly, I repeated what I'd heard.

"I've been able . . . to live . . . inside my calling." Done it despite all the day jobs and between and after them—always riding the full-tilt, gory carousel of human striving. Making work had shaped and driven and irradiated my days. My years. My being.

Wonderment flooded me—tantamount to Pinocchio's as he looks down at his newly fleshed body after a childhood made of wood.

My radio host, though I could not see him, must have been glowing. He'd blown his guest speaker's mind.

Get back, then, inner whiner!

The plain, innocent fact of the above, newly grasped reality, the blatant revelation of it—*always there* had I but stopped long enough to see, name, and embrace it—has been wagging a reminding finger at me ever since:

Remember this, my conscience murmurs—every single time you reflect upon that so-called saddest story ever told.

What Are We Afraid Of?

"The whole purport of literature . . . is the notation of the heart. Style is but the faintly contemptible vessel in which the bitter liquid is recommended to the world."

—THORNTON WILDER

Developing writers often seem consumed by fear. I watch their posts on social media. They fuss and angst and cringe. They venture, hesitate, hide; boast and preen, shrink and cower. They chafe and moan, begging for advice: what choices to make, paths to follow, names to tap, language to use. They recite personal stats in ornate detail: word counts, pages gathered, drafts wrangled, manuscripts sent. (Food and booze, illnesses and injuries in graphic close-up.) *Here's my infected toe! My broken arm/leg/nose! My black eye! Here's a photo of the stacked pages! OMG I pressed the Send button! Fix me a drink!*) They chronicle, for all to see, the tenor and timing of rejections.

They post their work's reviews, both praiseful and nasty. They tell their versions. They discuss their medications. They demand prayers and good vibes.

The fortune-cookie message folded inside all this contortionism, rain-dancing, forehead-smacking?

Somebody help me. I can't do this alone.

What's more, wish lists are explicit. *Tell me how not to blow it:*

whom to know, where to go, how to get magic. Give me luck. Give me love. Give me—

This insatiable need reminds me of the question posed to me by a young student in a long-ago undergrad writing class I was guest-lecturing.

Sitting in the front row, he'd been eyeing me with a silent skepticism I recognized and dreaded: there was never a way to satisfy those who scorned literary writing, a genre they found inscrutable and (because of its truthful reputation as nonlucrative) useless. They wanted to hear about the real payoff, the shortcut to glory, to Oprah, bestseller lists, big advances, film options. They felt sure I was holding back the formula.

"What do I have to do," this young man asked calmly, "to get my book onto the first shelf you see when you enter Barnes and Noble?"

For the record, I do understand there is a way to do that—get one's book displayed in a prime-visibility zone. But I never wanted to know more, because it seemed to involve (surprise) paying off somebody. It sounds dirty, though maybe it's no different from buying ad space. Still, no publisher of mine (all of them very small) could dream of affording such special placement. After the student stated his question I felt a familiar internal slump, which I had to pretend was not happening. I answered him in bland words about working hard. He rolled his eyes: *oh, please,* his clear message. *Get real.* My Girl Scouty response disgusted him. In fairness, his question did slam the unspoken yearning straight onto the table—forcing everyone in the room to stare at it:

I want to hit gold—get money, get a name—immediately. What are the steps?

I think about the student's confrontative question these many years later and see that in some ways social media still whiffs of it.

I also remember the years before the internet became the public bulletin board (what Hawaii used to call the Coconut Wireless) broadcasting writerly desire. Those years, if somewhat simpler, didn't feel much more restful or sane. In grad school I remember people becoming sick with dread when time came for them to read their work to a class or a workshop—even to dearest friends at happy hour: they went pale and shaky. To this hour, writers confront chopped nerves, stage fright, and panic attacks when it's time to perform— even the old pros; even online.

How—why—did it get this way?

Say we've decided (for the sake of this investigation) it's art we mean to make: Why, at the heart of the making, do we trust ourselves and our process so little? What is truly at risk for us?

No matter we're drowned by voices—real, recorded, on-screen, on paper. Written work still somehow stands as an ultra-raw, ultrapersonal piece of ourselves, even if the material was ghostwritten—even if it busies itself with nothing more risqué than gardening or recipes. Everyone feels the gods are watching every last semicolon, and like old Roman emperors will render eternal judgment on it. Whether through wildest imagination or unfiltered experience or both, written work has *come out of us*. Therefore it stands for us. We're offering our pound of flesh—some bones, too.

Given those stakes, starting out confused and scared makes sense. Few begin the serious practice of any discipline with gleaming nerve and confidence. Most beginning writers walk around dazed and sad. So do veteran writers, for that matter. Even celebrity writers routinely describe feeling utterly mystified by what they're doing, project after project. The notable difference between them and developing writers may be that the vets are not quite so susceptible to the opinions of others. But few are totally immune.

For myself, in the beginning? I remember feeling waves of terror that someone might at any moment call me a fraud—a wannabe masquerading as someone with real skill. Irrational, but true. And for a long time during those early years, it seemed to me that writers who taught—standard-bearers, curators—knew like Peter Pan how to fly. They'd been vetted. (Flying meant they could write with ease and conviction, and that the results would be uniformly glorious.) These teachers would *always* know how to fly; it was second nature. Further, they had the power and vision to anoint fledglings. And we students were auditioning for that—trying to convince the teachers and ourselves. We were the Darling kids. The trick—as Pan coached them—seemed to us a slippery matter of mind, of thinking right thoughts, not trying too hard while trying like hell. We secretly hoped our feigned ease—our effortful casualness—would create the necessary underdraft, or magic spark, to achieve lift-off.

I wondered for so long whether my feeling of groping blind—of clueless trying—would ever drop away.

It *sort of* did, after time. There was, naturally, a trade-off. At some point you noticed you simply had to give yourself permission to make what you wanted and do what you liked with it. But that self-conferred agency could also feel like a ball and chain—like being sentenced to the fetid back room of a small business, the lonely owner-operator staring at daily account columns, solely responsible for solvency. You gave yourself blanket permission to make your work, but then you had to agree to become everything else: editor, publicist, shrink, janitor—accountant.

And wow, was that marketplace competitive.

Nonetheless, the agency mentioned above, the permission? They're the heart of the deal. They *are* the deal.

As noted: it takes time.

For some, it takes little time. For others, permission's still out there, circling the airport.

Thus, the scratchy social media soundtrack: *Help me!*

But for those who've been at it awhile, high school angst about being seen with the right purse or hair or socks, or the coolest friends—has to have become a thing of the distant past. What exactly, then, are we still afraid of?

————

Let's first review the standard, starter anguishes, and how most writers have coped with them, to be able to put them aside.

A primal fear was always that of being called a bad writer: being told you lacked the goods. As a student I assumed (like most) that my work did not exist until someone in Authority said it did. Conversely, if Authority hated it, that meant my whole life and essence were nullified, too.

But after enough time in release from formal apprenticeship, the developing writer comes to see that very, very few are even paying attention. She figures out how to anoint herself—a sea change, by degrees. The developing writer also comes to accept that some readers will simply never *get* her work: will entirely miss or misread its soul and trajectory. (Amazon and similar review sites demonstrate this.) Writers learn to brace for that, and to slough it off like sand. Rather than let it contaminate them, they simply file the data—who will understand; who won't. This census becomes nearly impersonal, a clinical fact like terrain or weather. The writer learns to keep close to—and on good terms with—those who probably *will* get it.

We also grasp that nobody's an oracle, even heroes. Titans clash: so do their tastes. So do the tastemakers. Melville was excoriated for *Moby Dick*. Henry James hated *Tolstoy*. Critics sniffed at *Gatsby*. The list is very long. Behind-the-scenes jockeying and scuttlebutt churn and foam. Contemporary names blurb peers as a favor. Others diss or sell out peers because of jealousy, grudges, or the zeitgeist. Try Googling "legendary literary feuds" to view a boggling smorgasbord of them. The writer watches and listens to all this, and teaches herself to (mostly) shut out the roar.

Above all, the writer guards against internalizing it.

————

Rejection's always a humbug. Hearing "no" can wallop even the crustiest of us—whether from spouse, friends, relatives, lovers, fellow writers, teachers, editors, agents, publishers, or reviewers. We've all swum some portion of those cold, salty seas, or will. They're a natural part of the great triathlon of the life (Make, Sell, Represent). I speak from long history, and I have written at length elsewhere about rejection. Like daily sit-ups and push-ups, handling it seldom gets easier. The best we can manage is to make a routine chore of processing it.

In that spirit, I learned early to avoid workshops. (Apologies to my trillion friends who teach.) Though I weathered my share of them, placating a committee seemed a doomed tactic for writing. It worked best to ask just one or two trusted souls to look at new work. I'd also ask they please respond gently, while readying myself to discard unhelpful responses. Those people might not, I knew, be the right readers, never mind bearers of any last word. It would be crazy to give up because someone shrugged or wrinkled her nose. Damning torpedoes is part of the ongoing permission you give yourself. You bear down and push past. After a while you notice that even when someone you respected sniffed at it, the work somehow managed to find its way.

Rejection feels so embedded in the life that anyone staring long enough at its typical sequence (submit, be rejected, submit, be rejected) realizes there's no choice but to accept it as basic maintenance, like brushing teeth. Attitude keeps dread of rejection at bay. How? *By expecting it forever. Even if you become famous.* Again: we've no choice. Despair can paralyze. If we're paralyzed, nothing gets made. Literary taste is insanely subjective. (One editor adores, without fail, what another despises.) Thus, rejection's as inevitable as breathing. If you don't put the work out there, you're safe, but dead. If you put it out there, rejection's guaranteed—but *also, occasionally* sewn into its rough burlap lining like a tiny smuggled ruby, comes the rare, precious Yes.

We resolve, then, to harvest rejection; thresh it for anything useful, dump the chaff, repeat. As with any cyclical practice—farming, fishing, panning for gold, digging for the prize in the cereal box—our job's strictly to crank the Search along.

———

Alienating family and friends looms as a writerly fear—more for some than others. I hate saying this, but women seem extra vulnerable to it. It's not possible here to sift the millennia of wretched history making that so. To whatever degree women of every background and persuasion press ahead with life and art, Godspeed. Alienating people with our writing is, alas, real. I've done it. One offendee turned out to be my stepmother (now dead) to whom I felt—still feel—I owed nothing. Two others were friends whose feelings I'd ruffled, who forgave me later.

The risk of hurting others is real, but I continue to risk. This is not a brag: more a hapless admission. Because *what can be the point of dishonesty?* We have to tell as much hard truth as humanly possible. That's the work's defining nature. Why on earth otherwise take up this lonely, difficult, underpaid, ignored, often scorned, possibly soon-to-become-archaic avocation?

Here's a useful fact: most people don't read. Or: they don't read *your* stuff. They may vaguely remember liking what's-it-called by who's-their-name: that new thing with the shiny cover. I promise. If they actually read your work—heaven bless them. Mostly, very few will take in those pages. When some do, and then volunteer sincere thoughts about the work—even if they don't quite get it—hug them. Give them coffee, food, booze. Tell them you love them. Thank them glowingly, no matter what they said.

Friends who are bona fide friends will have some preliminary sense of why you are driven to write, of the complicated truth it demands—even if that's slightly beyond their understanding—and of how much their responses to your work will mean to you. If you fear losing them because of something you've written, you always have the choice of consulting them first to secure approval. (I have not done this and do not really believe in it, but some do and will.)

You decide.

I know one person who, many years ago, lost their entire family after a first, brilliant, wonderfully received novel in which the principal players may have been modeled on some of the author's family members. If I am perceiving right, that family completely shut out the author after the book's appearance. This gifted artist went on to make a new life with a new partner—possibly a better one than before. But loss of one's family cannot be a minor thing, and there's something biblically cruel to me about being cast out: such final vengeance, such cold impermeability—so powerful and deep it feels unbearably sad.

You would think this would persuade me not to risk it.

It can't.

Compunction to make truthful work may not prove pleasant for the fainthearted. Some would argue it's an illness.

I have no magic wisdom for warding off a possible outcome like the author's estrangement described above. You may have seen the inimitable Annie Lamott's famous quip: "You own everything that happened to you. Tell your stories. If people wanted you to write warmly about them, they should have behaved better."

Living with the aftermath, however, may be another matter.

Truth-telling in writing, including difficult fictive truth, is always terrifying. It's human to want to be loved. Yet truth-telling is fiction's job; literature's marrow. One doesn't elect to get into it to design pretty wallpaper. And art cannot stand as art if it's compromised. I have to believe in Graham Greene's splinter-of-ice-in-the-heart maxim—even if I haven't always adored Greene's applications of it.

———

Real writing—making it, performing it—for so long seemed to me, as noted, an ineffable thing just out of reach. It felt as though you had to osmose the *how* of it sideways, invisibly. When you finally managed a short hop (a piece that seemed to work), you might briefly feel aware of it, and even more briefly, glad and proud. But after that, bewilderingly, you found you could not carry over what you'd learned to the next project. You had to start from scratch again. You had to start from scratch: Every. Single. Time. What's more, the whole enterprise could disappear in a puff if you did not feed and care for it constantly.

It ain't restful.

And to come full circle, I see this precise torment playing out continuously. Degree programs, conferences. Retreats, boot camps, marathons. Covers of writers' magazines headlined with beckoning strategies, directories, competitions. Countless articles chant the same message—a message one wise author/teacher once summarized for her students this way:

It is possible to write.

Communing with fellow artists can sometimes feel lifesaving. More power to that; more power to whatever works. But despite all the shouting, writing that matters, in my view, simply *cannot be a social product or a hobby*. It cannot issue by committee or club, like a bake-off or a group craft collaboration. It's forged alone. Otherwise it's decor, pasteurized for safe consumption. (And if such is your jam, please thrive on. But it's not this inquiry's focus.)

Let's now summarize the standard fears just discussed, together with how the Late Work artist deals with them.

First, **fraud charges**: After years, self-permission gets granted and the work gets made.

Second, **rejection**: Time helps us understand it is coded into the process of making, its appearance a literal vital sign.

The third fear, **offending people**, forces us to face and take risks, hoping the worst won't happen—because without risk, the product forfeits its life as art.

What remains?

Dread of judgment looms reliably—that is, a writer's vulnerability to verdicts. Some swear they don't notice or care. I don't believe that. The world of making writing is so small; the spoils so bogglingly few. Mere *attention* to written work in our time is valued like gold, courted and fought over. Most authors coddle any particle of it—even as a pressed Like button. Many deny this, but I suspect we remember almost everything anyone ever wrote or said about our work. I can never forget a line from the first review of my first book (journalistic essays) in my region's metropolitan paper of record. The reviewer declared that the essays "go down like frozen yogurt." The implication was that they'd been contrived to ingratiate—like Easy Listening. It wasn't the worst thing anyone could say, yet it sliced me across the gut for its condescension.

But are we looking for charity when we send books into the world? Should we be entitled to expect a group hug?

Alas. I tell writing students: grow a dinosaur's skin. At the same time—so counterintuitively—we must write in large part from a skinless state. It's a bizarre, well-documented contradiction, a Jekyll–Hyde switch-up.

Performance anxiety partners review anxiety. The prospect of hitting the road (even virtually) on behalf of a new book makes some writers' hair fall out. True, the window of time for major publicizing is finite. Bookstores, virtual sessions: we get through it. Much is invented ad hoc. Alcohol may be deployed. The loving support of spouse and friends helps beyond saying.

So much for the Judgment hurdle.

———

Now we can move on to my main interest: areas not to fear, exactly, but that particularly and rather subtly challenge the late-work writer. By "late-work writer" I mean someone who by now carries a fairly clear (if rueful) understanding of their own patterns, strengths, and weaknesses; of the business end of the life as much as the internal world of it, and of the chasm between. The risks I next list will appear subtler and blurrier than those previously cited. They're harder to describe. They have most to do with locating and entering the work's true investigation.

By "risk" here I no longer mean threats of public embarrassment or private disaffection. I mean our own alertness to certain *aesthetic pitfalls* or craft potholes—a wrong turn, a dead end, an inadvertent shooting-one's-own-foot—that you and you alone can see.

The first that comes to mind is that of *lapsing into cleverness*. That sounds simplistic. But for people to whom language comes almost too easily, too swiftly and fluidly, avoiding easy cleverness becomes a deadly serious criterion and even—no exaggeration here—a moral responsibility. Cleverness can become, almost without one's noticing, a false god, a false gate—a lazy default, like drifting repeatedly over the center line on a highway. Cleverness cheats both writer and reader out of confronting the investigation's true heart by making tasty, distracting, camouflaging motions and sounds. Cleverness seduces because it promises relief from the discomfort of painful focus. The late-work writer knows she always remains hypersusceptible to interjecting the bon mot, the artful flourish—to toss handfuls of verbal sparkle into people's eyes and ears—hell, to toss them into her *own* eyes and ears.

She also knows this is a covert bid to nominate herself as a hero.

Donald Hall notes that Robert Frost once called Hall's then-Stanford professor Ivor Winters "clever, using the word as they use it at Oxford, to mean pretentious, shallow, callow, and meretricious."

The clear and omnipresent mission? Distrust cleverness. Push against the instinct and whenever it sneaks through, hunt its effects down and cut them away. Grip that impulse with both hands—it's crazy strong—and hold it still till it's subdued. As you go, keep hacking off all pretty decoys until you arrive to the difficult, homelier truth.

Then, somehow, try to enter that.

Again and again I find myself reading work that sounds the way I imagine its author speaks in casual conversation—droll, lofty, self-ironic. My heart always falls then, and I can feel myself losing belief in the voice. The material may be witty and charming—but odds are it has strayed from the heart of its intent, sometimes precisely because it is so funny and smart. (I hasten to add: this doesn't mean brave literary art can't be funny. Think of *Lucky Jim* or *Straight Man*; of Lorri Moore or Laurie Colwin. But wit, qua wit, can't generally be enough.)

Cleverness may please a writer moments after it's issued. But soon—almost every time—it will sound like quacking. Self-admiring, strutty—thin and flaky as peeling paint. That's how cleverness quickly sounds to the reading ear. All you need to do, scanning pages, is look for the sound of quacking. You'll find it. Then you'll know what to do.

So killing cleverness is among the mature writer's first (yet constant) jobs.

By now we know the bottom-line fear for writers: loss of health and, above all, acuity of mind. You've got to be able to sit up, look clearly at the sentences, assimilate them, and think. Perhaps the cleverness reflex serves as a kind of auto-defense against that bony, cloaked spirit breathing heavily at your shoulder, gripping its scythe: *Back off*, you want to shout at it. *I'm fine. My mind's sound—zingy in fact.* But *zingy* can wind up sabotaging the careless artist, spiraling her sideways—black ice on which the project may spin out.

We refine the gaze, crank up the magnification, sharpen the axe.

———

A second principle of what the late-work maker looks out for and guns against is *inauthenticity*. A chewy word—but it gets its job done. Is the thing we are trying to frame, to isolate and palpate, the real inquest? Or are we, with our words and thoughts, doing some seven-veils dance to entice ourselves away from it, swirling diaphanous scarves around the real freak-out? (I'm reminded of a scene from the original *Ghostbusters* movie: Sigourney Weaver opens her refrigerator and faces a horned demon screaming at her from a flaming maw. She shuts it fast.)

We are charged—we *charge ourselves*—with chasing down the unspeakable: exposing, naming, dissecting, detonating it. There have been periods of working with material so agonizing to me I had to get up and sit down and twist this way and that to pop bones and itch and scratch and yawn and rub my eyes and eat and drink and nap and sigh and maunder, brood and stare at online idiocy and waste absurd numbers of hours on peripheral nonsense—everything short of punching myself in the face to get the painful scenes told, the right words said, the principals from one room or city to the next or one decade to the next. This is not boasting. It felt miserable. It felt hopeless, lost, tumbling-down-a-cold-well lonely.

But I couldn't not do it.

Nobody forced me. Nobody cared, or even knew it was happening. No reason they should. It would have been better if someone *had* tried to force me so I could hate them and blame them for everything. There was only the interior troll to blame, the small-business boss insisting I had to inventory *all* the shelves before I could go home and sleep the sleep of the just. I can't feel heroic about it. Others will handle these trials better—more briskly, smartly, courageously—less bleatingly. I'm mainly relieved I didn't just blow off the ordeals and wander away, or drink or drug myself blind and fall off a bridge. The things that needed to get told, finally got told. They're in the world. With any luck they'll outlive me a bit. A certain peace seeps through my body in the wake of that, a calm spentness something like Dickinson's *formal feeling.* I'm also aware that surviving one wrestling match won't make the next any easier—not one speck easier. I can't think too long about that. Maybe it's like childbirth—you can't let yourself think about the harshest parts until it's too late.

———

If authenticity means facing down the nasty thing in the woodshed, it may also mean relinquishing a favored habit—of focus, ideation, or style. Writers may so fall in love with a notion or turn of phrase, we can't let go of it. I am often guilty of this—also (in the style department) of offering far too many analogies. More than one reader has accused me of inventing seven doors for getting into the same room.

Ouch.

Any literary writer, at whatever stage but most emphatically in late years, eventually sees that the supreme concern must be that of *continuing to surprise herself*—to reach further, push deeper, discern more finely, pry loose the unnoticed or unexamined, allow weird newness or new weirdness. Even the best of us resist that. It becomes the late-work writer's steady, perhaps subtlest, challenge. "I don't want to repeat myself, but I don't want to change that much," admitted the great Joan Silber during an online conversation. Her remark actually gave me heart. Each work we make is a one-off mystery. Finding our way through each is always unprescribable. Choices comprise craft: that's all we know. Maps, however well intended, cannot rule. ("The map is not the territory," notes my author/teacher friend, quoting a famous psychiatrist.)

In the words of the wonderful, late poet William Stafford: "More, there is more." But you can't know what *more* will consist of, most of the time, until you're swimming for your life in it. That's the joy and throwdown, the mixed-nuts fallout of the life: reason to despair and equally, heaven help those of us doomed to it, reason to lean in and start riffling around. What's behind Door Number Three? How did the cosmos look before it was made?

It is possible to write.

It Seemed Important at the Time:
The New Doubt

"He wrote . . . not to be remembered but to be read, the only goal within his reach."

—MIKE PRIDE, "DONALD HALL'S LATE BURST OF CREATIVITY,"
THE NEW YORKER

"Our doubt is our passion and our passion is our task."

—HENRY JAMES, "THE MIDDLE YEARS"

H ello. My name is Joan, and I'm a doubt-wrangler.
   After a lifetime of writing, a brazen sense of its meaningless-ness has shot me in the back.

Practitioners may scoff at this as super-old news—something that, if you've not managed to muzzle it by now, too bad for you.

Yet it has loomed, haunting my hours, and shows no signs of going away.

Stubborn. Puzzling. Also an encumbrance, like a Denver boot.

It's not that reading doesn't still rock. I read hungrily, scanning for miracles; for the voice that punches into my chest, murmuring *Hear this now*, or *Yes, I know exactly*. And I still do find those voices—in different forms, personalities, eras. If I go out to perform an errand that involves waiting (car wash, doctor's office), I still panic if I've for-gotten to bring a book. And when I scroll through social media, my heart never fails to beat harder when it finds posts by or about my favorite authors.

So what's my problem?

Why have I begun to question what good my own (or much contemporary) writing may do? Why does a huge portion of the industry, and the multiform hype surrounding it, now seem an avalanche of empty noise? Why do I experience a creeping numbness, after years of feeling driven? What happened to my cold hands and pounding heart before readings; to that delicious *on-the-path* rush for a new project?

This is not to whine, sulk, or beg. It's more a truth blurt. While never wishing to insult my writing and teaching friends—they are many—these days I can't quite own the same force of *mattering*. (Classics still carry oomph—but slightly dimmed, slightly flattened, as if run over by a truck. Austen, James, Baldwin, the great poets—heavy hitters whose every semicolon I've enshrined—now sound muted and blurry, as if intoning underwater.)

I have misplaced my mojo—though it's still true that almost every day someone tells me (or I tell myself), *you should write about this.*

Something has shifted.

Yes, there's the small matter of nearly three COVID years. It may be more accurate to recast the shift as atmospheric—a kind of bog-fog wafting from colluding elements of time and the pandemic. The latter, of course, has left its mark on everyone—some much more horribly than others—and at this hour remains far from over. I see (from their posts) the same fog confounding other artists. Some admit it straightaway, sad, adrift. Others swear that lockdown (and the known world being canceled) only charged them up more. I distrust those claims. If the Earth's been put on notice it's about to disintegrate, will a logical first response be to sharpen pencils? Maybe, for some. Either way, few have escaped a sense of being forced to reassess and redefine a relationship to what they do.

For me, clarity and conviction took a tremendous hit.

Reading's lost some luster. True—the industry gushes with new titles, some of which I review for major venues, and I still grab three or four of them at a pop for personal consumption. Yet I've watched my own attention ebb and twitch, restless, jumpy, and I confess here without naming names that I return many of those titles to the library after reading perhaps thirty pages. Rarely now comes the old hunker-down fixation with a book that kept me up too late. Instead, trying to focus feels like trying to start a stalled car. Interruptions bombard— or I leap up to seek them. My sense of what I've read smears. Too often I have to reread lines. Yes, others have described their pandemic-altered habits—lost concentration—in these ways. Yet in my own case I sense that quarantine cannot take all the blame.

Not long ago I skimmed through the late poet James Wright's collected letters, *A Wild Perfection*. Allowing for the mess of my own heart and mind, and with all respect for the timeless power of Wright's art—these pages struck me as a great pile-on of perfunctory wit and worry; of Wright doing what we all do in letters, which is to recite the daily: travel, jobs, family, projects. Nothing rang *false* about those recorded thoughts; it seemed to be the sheer routineness of their concerns (windfalls, reversals, minutiae) that dismayed me. Why? Because all of it happened years ago—and because I recognized myself; my own present-tense minutiae. This further depressed me. Who can ignore the obvious oblivion mirrored in the minutiae of others' letters, toward which our own homely lives are headed; details that seemed so important at the time?

(Again, this is not to diminish or sideline the great Wright's gifts.)

I'm today about twenty years older than Wright lived to be. And despite alcohol having so damaged and probably shortened his life, he remained a staunch Believer. Even when wrecked, he scarcely wavered from Van Gogh's "seeking . . . searching . . . in it with all my heart." (One biographer notes that at lowest ebb Wright began to jot a suicide note, then got sidetracked by the possible use of its language for a poem.) In final years Wright maintained sobriety, working intensely and well—luckily for us all.

I don't quite understand why reading those letters threw me so hard. I had sought the collection with eagerness because I'd been thrilled by *The Strength and Delicacy of Lace*, a slender exchange of letters between Wright and the poet Leslie Marmon Silko, published by Wright's widow after his death. That conversation felt timeless, enchanting, piercingly human. As I recall, the two often focused upon the raw emotional terrain of artmaking—*what am I doing; what is to become of me, does my work have anything*, and so on. Poignant, personal markers emerge—Silko loses a custody battle; her chickens are swept off by a coyote; Wright's relationship with his sons grows painful.

Maybe the angst prompted by Wright's major collection had to do with noticing that *any* itemized dailiness from past eras can't help quickly sounding tinny, parochial, small. God knows I've sounded that way in letters all my life—while striving to impress, to present as fresh and nervy, spilling bon mots. *Love me for how smart I sound*, may as well have been written below each line. And this in turn makes me wonder whether (short of a lobotomy) there's ever a way to scotch that insatiable longing, at the root, to be loved. Shouldn't the reflex be replaced, as an artist enters Late Work years, by some restraint, some humility—some droll self-possession? Shouldn't those traits be installed by then? Or does craving love simply continue to drive us, no matter the age or work?

While reading them, I could only perceive Wright's letters (with apologies and more respect) as less a plea to be loved than a bulwark of busy noise. But what most mashed me was grasping that the letters and all they dreamed, all they tried to be and do, would be fast and thoroughly forgotten—except by a curious, devoted, or scholarly handful.

My husband reminds me that when a once-famous local painter died, his adult children gathered to clean out his house. They gave a few of his paintings to a nearby museum—and tossed the rest into a dumpster.

Surely this has always been the tacit reality of artmaking. As noted, it's hardly new news. The late, inimitable Donald Hall, in his superb compendium *Old Poets: Reminiscences & Opinions*, compares the vagaries of literary taste and legacies to the rise and fall of the stock market. He offers a number of martini-dry observations: "Writers with enormous followings in their own lifetimes go unread and unmentioned a generation later. . . . [Whatever made a work adored in its time] proves not available to subsequent eras; it wanders the heavens like a dead spaceship, cold and dark. . . . It is sensible to assume that the taste of our own moment will come to seem fatuous, including yours and mine."

I love that dead spaceship.

But Hall's wisdom didn't make the Wright business go away. What was the point of any of our striving and scrambling? Can you imagine that Wright—or Hall, or any living artist we esteem—would care about how many Likes a thing gets?

One understands rationally that Wright's poetry stands apart for itself: unalloyed, golden. Anyone, now or later, may or may not know he existed. Anyone may elect to study his work, now or in a hundred years. But if humans continue to exist, we know his work will abide— serenely. It has no plane to catch.

Maybe the visible disjunction between a maker's art and personal life over years effects the kind of quandary some of us face when read- ing even ultra-famous people's letters—filled as they often are with familiar dailiness: toil, finagling, domestic anguish. Why, a reader may soon wonder, am I needing to know this?

Maybe it's just the hard fact that the letters are old. Remember the feeling of discovering piles of old postcards at a flea market? Recall the fluttering in your stomach as you scanned the guileless, hand- scripted messages posted from some long-mummified boarding house or hotel? Recall that same flutter, coming upon the carefully fountain-penned inscriptions in the front pages of aged books— *Merry Christmas, Happy Birthday, 1927*?

More confoundingly: I've only recently shaped a euphoric piece about the concrete joys of letter-writing: the erotic richness of the form, its perfect freedom, even the cathartic release of letting e-letters vanish like sand-painting into the ethersphere. For this reason, too, suddenly experiencing Wright's letters as small, even immaterial, feels confusing and uncomfortable. Shouldn't I be able to see and imagine more generously—deferring to the obvious cycle of all of us?

A man, a woman, lived, died. They made some art.

Yet all I can think lately, confronting such collections, is: What or whom, besides some few scholars, can this finally serve?

The question echoes back at me about everything I've ever done.

And as the pandemic's course zigzags in North America and (somehow) an intensified torrent of books, events, and reviews rushes at me, the accelerating clamor makes me want to run away—or hit the Delete button (then voluptuously, satisfyingly, empty the e-trash).

This is not normal. I should rejoice at literary life's renewed energy. For most of my adult years I've lived in a hyperalert state of attunedness to the range of it—who's making and reading what, all the stories and gossip—the whole food chain.

That fund of care feels hollowed, flattened.

What should any artist in their Late Work years—anyone in final years—reasonably want?

And why don't the usual answers to this question—health, love, good work—feel like quite enough just now?

To appease the default nihilists among us, and for deck-clearing's sake: Let's cheerfully assume that in fact *no one* is paying attention, or really ever was, for good measure. Let's say there was a *never* a genuinely good time for art, unless you'd managed to clamber onto the Medici payroll. Let's say that currently everyone's watching a bake-off show, or Insta or TikTok. Or they're fishing or doing laundry or childminding or working three jobs. What, besides staying alive, proves worth following? What's worth holding close?

I do not ask these questions disingenuously. A wise man long ago suggested that "everything is exactly what you hold it to be."

But what if your own, self-applied meanings start to peel off and fall away like wet Band-Aids?

I've mentioned the New Doubt once or twice to a select few. A couple of polite acquaintances only stared at me. (Bless them: I hadn't expected more.) But when I told my dearest, most trusted writing friends they were not only not surprised—they didn't try to deny or correct what I'd described. They recognized it because they'd experienced some form of it themselves. Why pretend otherwise? Why lie about the sad drooly bony smelly Black Dog plopping down upon one's chest at all hours, groaning and farting in its nightmare-riddled sleep?

A kinder, pluckier description of the New Doubt might be to call it a Wider Vision (often delivered by that generous agent, time). Like a stretched-horizontal photo of a cityscape or a landscape, the term suggests a more panoramic view—in this case, that of the simultaneity of conflicting truths: *One accepts that making work cannot durably matter.* That is, one knows one's products will dissolve almost instantly into invisibility, like sugar in water.

And one keeps making work.

Notice the "and" as opposed to any "but."

In short, one can't *not* make work. (In author Charles Baxter's wonderful words, fuck and alas.) Please know that saying this is one thing. Feeling it in full context is another. You've probably heard the phrase *can't not* on plenty of occasions—and felt your annoyed reasoning do the tiny backflip required to absorb it. Inexplicably, it's a default function quite outside personal will, like the shin bouncing when a doctor taps the knee.

Oh, Twilight Zone–ish fate! Writers as wind-up dolls who can only totter straight off cliffs.

The nature of time would seem to insist upon it.

"No honest poet can ever feel quite sure of the permanent value of what he has written," noted T. S. Eliot during an interview with Donald Hall, in the above-mentioned essay collection. "He may have wasted his time and messed up his life for nothing." Hall adds: "Maybe no one ambitious, in any line of work, dies with conviction of accomplishment." Elsewhere, author Will Self has quipped: "Every writer . . . must acknowledge their works' limited shelf-life as well as their own mortality. With so many more books and writers—[and] appreciably fewer serious readers, surely there's going to be a lot less posterity to go round."

Yet we persist. To restate the case for safekeeping: *one keeps making work while clearly understanding that the results will vanish.* It's finally not a million miles from the way we keep getting up in the morning with the irrefutable knowledge that one day, we won't. We go ahead and get up. It's all we've got.

This comprehension fairly cancels most swashbuckling notions of heading into battle, Musketeer-like, for some brave moral principle, or to defend art's honor.

The reality feels more like laying one's head down on the glass plate where a breast gets inserted for a mammogram, at the moment when another plate positioned over it gets cranked down tightly upon it to flatten it. Except it's your head. Sorry.

Also? It turns out the New Doubt hasn't much to do with nostalgia for a bygone, golden era—though it may think it does, at first. I did for some time believe a more just era once existed (vaguely, the 1940s to 1950s). This is still argued—still longed for, in some circles. But evidence suggests the impression was, at best, overrated. Cases may be made for various writers in prior periods achieving better visibility, better pay, better recognition while they lived. Some did manage to make a living at it. Some got rich. (Check the YouTube of Margaret Mitchell blinking in flashbulb lights at the glittering 1939 Atlanta premiere of her novel's film version. And of course, there are individuals today making millions.) But most, of course, didn't, and won't. I would guess that now, even as publishing morphs into four monster-conglomerates while zillions of aspiring writers toil away dreaming of gold (and zillions more stand poised to replace them), the relative difficulty of the gig never fundamentally alters. Even those stars we assume to have been brilliantly successful endured bitter trials. Most grappled with blockages, torments, injustices— even the wealthy. Too often, fame came posthumously.

Maybe the New Task, responding to the New Doubt, is to invent a fresh mantra. Language still fires and organizes us, despite our cynicism. Here's a telling excerpt from poet Robert Hass's remarks during an interview (italics are mine):

One of the things that was interesting to me working with Czeslaw [the late, Nobel-winning poet Czesław Milosz] for twenty-five years was that *he never thought it wasn't the most important thing in the world.* He had despair about the world. He had despair about whether his art could ever achieve what he hoped it would achieve. He had a feeling that serious art can lose its way among junk. But he always felt that, as he says in one poem, "Great was that chase with the hounds for the unattainable meaning of the world." He always thought that the poets and the philosophers and the artists and the theologians and so forth were engaged in the grand human adventure.

These are glorious words. For a moment one can feel them lifting one up by the armpits. Yet (gently sliding back down) I can no longer argue with my whole heart for that great chase. Once it felt bracing and apt to tie up discussions like this one with a fist-thumping-into-palm Yes. Now I would probably sigh and squint off into the distance, trying to cherry-pick the language that could most kindly warn off aspiring writers. I would feel that they deserved that courtesy—*unless* they'd already demonstrated self-esteem made of steel, understood they could never quit a day job (or supporting partner), and knew in their bones they were incapable of doing anything else.

A wise friend, hearing these thoughts, sent a perfect quote from Oscar Wilde:

"Art, like life, is utterly unnecessary."

Meantime, I keep staring at a phrase I sent a couple of close friends during darkest hours:

I really don't know how else to be.

Inside that assertion, please notice a sneaky assumption: I must *not want to know* how else to be. Other options always exist. *You can always—just—stop.* Yet some internal jury denies this option, with zero deliberation. The recoil is practically physical. Why? Because in the internal jury's opinion, *being about anything else is, for all purposes, death by suffocation.* To confront the idea of quitting is to be sent around the world to the back of your own head in fractions of seconds. Life *without* thinking it through, by way of writing? Infeasible. It's a way of assimilating—even what's theoretically non-assimilable. A way of being, nearly as vital as breathing.

This awareness proves impossible to erase, reverse—*or* to convey in civil society without offending somebody.

What other pursuit regards itself and the human predicament so intra-dimensionally—so expansively, deeply, wryly? (I'm hearing the music of words from "Dover Beach:" *So various, so beautiful, so new.*) What other avocation musters such patient self-irony while also acting out in raw, sweaty earnestness? What other gig lends perceived existence such shape-shifting pith and scope and momentum and even, somehow, wit?

Above all: If you gave it up, what would be left?

Mindful, again, that what we make gets washed away: If we could devise a more gratifying (not remunerative, not even rewarding—but gratifying) preoccupation, would we not have long ago set off in a heartbeat to find it—whistling?

This curious standoff might best be distilled in a scene from the 1966 art-house film *King of Hearts*. In it, a young Scottish soldier (Alan Bates) arrives to a small French town that's been abandoned by its citizens, after wartime fighting's left it booby-trapped. Bates has been assigned to find a bomb set to go off there by the Germans.

The town's insane-asylum inmates, a ragtag lot, have escaped their confinement and wander the streets blissfully. Bates's soldier, figuring out when the bomb will blow but unable to disarm it, strives without success to round up these hapless innocents and hustle them out of there.

They don't understand. They find his urgency touching, and go on about their dreamy business. One fellow, I seem to recall, likes to hold a velvet ribbon against his cheek.

At last, Bates's frantic soldier accosts the luminously beautiful, mad young ballerina (Genevieve Bujold), grappling for words to make her realize they must flee at once; destruction is imminent.

They have, he shouts at her, only six minutes before the explosion.

She searches his face with her enormous, lovely, dark eyes.

"Six minutes," she murmurs, her eyes never leaving his. "Yes. It's wonderful!"

The Action Figures Collection

In an essay for *American Theatre* magazine, playwright Craig Lucas (*Prelude to a Kiss*) described finding himself, some years ago, in the middle of a kind of personal renaissance, having just received a wonderful award.

Lucas had been given the Greenfield Prize. That meant a $30,000 stipend and a writing residence at a place called the Hermitage in Englewood, Florida. His life, he cheerfully admitted, was a mess at the time: his marriage done, his work dead-ended. Though he'd overcome alcoholism and addiction, he wasn't sure, at sixty, "what kind of character I wanted to play in my third act."

The retreat and cash prize gave him what every writer craves: time, space, financial stability. He could sort himself out and make new work. In what feels like a report or evaluation of this windfall experience, his essay tries to convey "the one big surprising thing I learned in my year of reading, contemplation and conversations with the Hermitage staff and fellow artists."

I reread his essay several times, struggling to summarize for myself that "one big surprising thing." I sensed that Lucas had written the piece in a heightened state, even perhaps a fugue state. That is to say, he was quite high—a recognizable art-colony high, that supremely fertile, alert, all-pores-open period when the very air seems to vibrate and the imagination with it. During that time, delicious possibilities rise to the surface like glistening golden carp, promising to coalesce into something brilliant—if we can just string together the words to finesse the job.

Lucas was high on the freedom and peace of a solitude that's supported and protected by like-minded others, unimpinged upon by interruptions and demands. He felt he was glimpsing, during that high, What It All Means, and he tries in this essay to tell us: "Self-knowledge. . . . Trust in others, time, process. . . . Humility and gratitude [are key] in gaining mastery. . . . I can't afford the luxuries of self-pity and resentment, privileging me and my work over others." Bad reviews, he adds, "are like weather . . . a permanent condition of being an artist." In fact, he declared, bad reviews have freed him "to write what I might otherwise have feared to say."

"Art models freedom," he notes, "but you must choose it—and keep choosing it."

That got my attention.

"We are what we do, not what we say, feel, or intend," he adds.

Lucas sensed that the constant trick of making art is to resist being dragged under by "gossip and schadenfreude." Act in aggressive *opposition* to those reflexes, he suggests. Better art will follow.

When I read this essay, it both touched and bothered me. I understood its circumstances, and admired its earnestness. Lucas's urgency, surely hard-earned, was inspiring. Yet from experience I know how that foamy, effervescent high in artistic retreat (with all its passionate revelations) can soon evaporate as we return to the daily, as we resume trying to fit writing in amid chores and obligations—ducking the slings and arrows.

I also recognize that art that matters—rather, art that winds up mattering, since time is the only real arbiter of that—can come from awful people. The books we write are not us, finally—for better and occasionally for worse.

But lately I've begun to suspect that Lucas, and others like him, may be onto something—something almost chemical—about giving back, "contributing to the common good" and "acting in opposition" to mean or petty reflexes.

Believe me: I'm the last person I'd expect to hear saying this.

After more time in the life than I like to concede, I've only recently started to figure out (slow learner) that crabby, covetous fretting hasn't done a lot to help my work's success. My *work* has helped my work's success (combined with rabid determination to send it out to as many pairs of eyes as may be willing to glance at it). So has the unstinting generosity of several generations of superb teachers and writing mentors.

Increasingly, in fact, a habitually gloomy attitude strikes me as deadweight: stale, boring, cumbersome, and—most interestingly— irrelevant. Of no use at all.

At the same time, we've all noticed over the years that there are writers out there whose generosity and kindness are so legendary as to form a sizable piece of their identities. Certain names stand out as synonyms for "amazing goodness." Their reflexive graciousness seems to so shockingly transcend (even disprove) the street-level grit and grime of the writing life—the thousand-and-one frustrations and jealousies, the scraping and scrabbling—that we remember them for it.

You've doubtless met some of the people I'm talking about. The encounter always feels astonishing. They look you in the eye. They offer clear, sensible words of encouragement, and appear to mean it. They follow through with the help they pledged, the referral, the recommendation letter, the blurb. They cheer for you when good things happen for your work. And they seem to manage all this without visible strain, guilt-mongering, or similar complexities—whatever else they may be juggling in their own lives—year after year.

In short, their integrity seems real.

Lucas grasped, I think, that this mind-set (and behavior) works as an antidote to almost everything that can discourage us about the writing life—everything that *can make us waste precious time* questioning ourselves, and it.

Therefore, I want to be like those writers. Or at least to bear them in mind, talismanically.

Something along the lines of a mental bumper sticker:

What would (name inserted here) do?

What if it helped us, as artists, to keep a sort of private roll call of these exemplars in the backs of our minds—like a collection of those action figures we used to play with as kids, hopping them around on furniture, giving them voices (though of course the mortal models for these figures have well-established voices), telling stories with them?

The writers I'm thinking of are in no way, let me hasten to add, Pollyannas. They know the game well. They've seen all the trends and cycles. They've wished for the same things we've wished for, that the life parses out so grudgingly: recognition, critical approval, a bit of money. They've been burned; even encountered rejection. Imagine!

So when I propose this, I don't mean to candy-coat the difficulties and pitfalls of the life. Also, I do not imagine I can fool the universe into thinking I'm a nice person. The universe is smarter than that— and being a nice person, as noted earlier, doesn't automatically make good art. (Jane Smiley once quipped, in a list of writing tips, that "you cannot know human variety and maintain good manners at the same time.")

What I have in mind is at least an effort to reroute a reflex. Even if the stellar models have been faking it all this time, something got sparked by that. Function follows form to a stupendous degree. Spirit follows letter. *We are what we do, not what we say.* So whether inside or outside the haven of artistic retreat, no matter how my inner curmudgeon groans, I'll try more, in days ahead, to emulate the words and especially the *deeds* of my action figures collection.

I, too, am curious about how that third act turns out.

Coda: Someone Is Reading

"It's so easy to think you don't matter all that much at the very moment when your moral duty as a self is most exposed."

—RACHEL CUSK

"I plan to continue living. That's the central idea."

—PAUL MCCARTNEY

Stephen Sondheim's beloved musical *Into the Woods* features a heart-slicing song called "Children Will Listen," in which his singer warns:

> *Careful the things you say*
> *Children will listen . . .*
> *Careful the things you do*
> *Children will see and learn . . .*

This haunting, bittersweet, cautionary song has rested softly in memory years after I heard it performed, until a recent event pushed it forward again.

Its syllables—its caution—echo something a kind friend remarked after I'd been thrown into an illogical depression.

The funk was triggered when I received word that a small literary prize was being awarded to a book of mine. No money was involved: just the distinction of the work's being singled out. Of course I felt, and remain, grateful. But I also grew sad. What overwhelmed me was the smallness of the event; its near-instant erasure from anyone's radar—pushed quickly out to sea alongside the daily tidal debris of other news.

But my wise and lovely friend—himself an emeritus of artmaking in a different medium, who occasionally also broods about his own effectiveness in his field—said something like this: "At least [the award] shows that someone is reading." He went on, very kindly, to compliment that reader's taste.

The phrase *someone is reading* echoed in my mind's ear—partly because its syllables and rhythm exactly match those of *children will listen*, the Sondheim song's title and refrain. More urgently, it struck me that a parallel message ran inside the two observations, a wisdom that carries across artistic media, beyond its application to literary work. Rather than further saddening me the phrase began, slowly, to turn things around. The words reminded me (and continue to remind me) that despite the great welter of any artist's despair about what their work may ever mean—*someone is reading (listening, watching)*. That is: someone somewhere is taking in that work.

Those specific someones may not number many. And their tastes might not be ours. But they are real, and taking to heart what they hear, see, and read. It's entering them. It's *news* for them. At some level it will be absorbed into them and carried along like DNA ever after; sometimes, also, passed on. ("You've *got* to read this, listen to this, watch this.")

An author friend once noted that in her own mind she writes for *one other* secret friend—a fantasized bestie reading the work under the covers, by flashlight.

Someone is reading.

I know this without question, because of course I've spent my already—luckily long life doing exactly that—still a certified member of that club of pensive someones. Listening, watching, reading. Being infused, sometimes life-changingly, by what I heard or saw. And there's no quantifying the gift to all those waking hours and days and years of music, art, and literary glory: enrichments that have simply made all the difference. It's not too much to say they have formed me.

―――――

Sometimes they have saved me, in blackest intervals. Once I worked at a self-service gas station on a hot, noisy interstate, the only job I could find after leaving the Peace Corps and moving in with my adored younger sister, whose husband, tragically, had just been suddenly killed in a sledding accident. I read the entire *Sherlock Holmes* series at that gas station job, enthralled and carried far away from the harsh noise of speeding cars and sorrow. In Cefalu, Sicily, Anthony Trollope came to my rescue, somehow draping the ancient, hardscrabble surroundings (which carried a patina of poverty and desolation) with the rich, heavy brocade of a different era. Its story cossetted me while making me more aware of the world's polyphonic evolution, a kind of counterpoint. I remember being electrified and consoled during many lonely years by certain then-obscure works—Marilynne Robinson's *Housekeeping* or Joan Chase's *During the Reign of the Queen of Persia* or Shirley Hazzard's *The Transit of Venus* or Anne Michaels's *Fugitive Pieces* or William Maxwell's *So Long, See You Tomorrow* or Tove Jansson's *The Summer Book* or J. L. Carr's *A Month in the Country* or Robert Seethaler's *A Whole Life*. Earlier, Baldwin's *Giovanni's Room*, Rhys's *Wide Sargasso Sea*, Kinkaid's *Annie John*, the indelible works of childhood—eerie, brave testaments that live inside one all one's days like a remembered dream. And when stumbling through England in blind, stupid grief after losing my only beloved sister herself, how sorely grateful I felt for the nightly comfort and wisdom of David Constantine's novel *The Life-Writer*. Looking back, these titles (and so many more) seem to connect beneath the surface like islands: to stem from a single awareness—incandescent with an understanding of the near-inexpressible. Which in turn surely has everything to do with what Thornton Wilder called the eternal—the aura that feels wrapped around the wretched, niggling chaos of human experience. Can you imagine a life without books, films, paintings, sculpture, music?

Someone is reading.

Some of those readers, too—praise heaven—are actual children. Some of them grow up to keep reading. That's how we become ourselves. And I know that the fact of those stalwart, singular someones persists out there, despite the incalculable horror and bedlam of concurrent culture, because occasionally people write to me to tell me they were reached into, even altered a little, by something I made that they read. And of course I write to thank those living authors who've reached into me and changed me. Nine times out of ten they write back gratefully. They're one of those someones who are reading, too.

The song goes on:

> *Careful the spell you cast*
> *Not just on children*
> *Sometimes the spell may last*
> *Past what you can see*

"Things can happen" when a book ventures into the world, declared author Margot Livesey. Someone will always be reading. If I am still reading, reason suggests, so, too, are others. And this, in the sum of its promise and fact, is what the writer, all her days, must believe and return to again and again.